George MacDonald, Cullen, and Malcolm

A VICTORIAN LITERARY PORTRAIT OF 1870s CULLEN

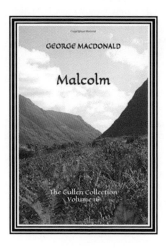

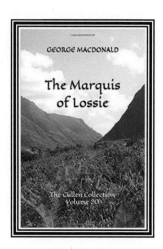

by
Michael & Judy Phillips

In Memory of
GEORGE MACDONALD (1824-1905)

Huntly native, best-selling author,
one of Scotland's 19th century spiritual bards,
and lifelong lover of Cullen

*To research his newest fictional project, MacDonald returned to
this favourite region of boyhood memories during the years 1872
and 1873. During these visits, he stayed at the Seafield Arms
Hotel, at a manse in Deskford, in a house on Grant Street, and
visited Cullen House. Many local tales from residents and
fishermen were later fictionalised in the pages of MacDonald's
memorable companion novels set in Cullen and its environs—
MALCOLM (1875) and THE MARQUIS OF LOSSIE (1877).*

*A thank you goes to many individuals on both sides of the pond for their
proofreading of the booklet and for many other valuable suggestions. A
special thanks to Marian McPherson and Duncan Wood (author of Cullen:
Records of a Royal Burgh and Cullen A Pictorial History) for many of the
photographs used, including Marian's cover photo.*

—Michael and Judy

"Papa seems so quietly happy."
—Louisa MacDonald, May 4, 1872, from Deskford (near Cullen)

"Papa does enjoy this place so much."
—Louisa MacDonald, May 6, 1872 from the Seafield Arms Hotel

"Papa oh! so jolly & bright & happy…Papa was taken for Lord Seafield yesterday."
—Louisa MacDonald, Sept. 2, 1873, from Cullen

"Papa is very poorly. He ought to go to Cullen for a week I think."
—Louisa MacDonald, October 5, 1873, from London

Contents

View from "New Churchyard" (cemetery adjacent to caravan park) showing Castle Hill in the foreground of the two Bins with the mast of the market cross faintly visible. The market cross had been built outside the gates of the Auld Kirk and was moved to Castle Hill in 1821 when the old town was demolished during the 1820s. It remained there until 1872 when it was incorporated into the gothic structure that we see in the Square today. It is possible that George MacDonald may have witnessed the building of the new market cross in the Square on his first visit to Cullen in 1872.—*Duncan Wood*

Cullen's Castle Hill and George MacDonald Memorial Bench

Famed Victorian Novelist
George MacDonald Visits Cullen

Scottish Victorian novelist, preacher, poet, and spiritual bard George MacDonald had a lifetime regard for Cullen and the surrounding area. A native of Huntly, with family ties to Portsoy and Banff, all his life MacDonald cherished fond memories of his childhood in northeast Scotland and holidays at the sea in Cullen.

In preparation for the books he planned to write set in Banffshire, MacDonald sojourned to Cullen in successive years, in the late spring of 1872 and again in the autumn of 1873. In addition to visiting Cullen house, he stayed at the Seafield Arms Hotel, at the Free Church manse in Deskford, and lodged for a time on Grant Street where a portion of the initial writing of *Malcolm* took place. *Malcolm* was serialised in the *Glasgow Weekly Herald* in 1874 and published in book form in 1875. It was followed in 1877 by *The Marquis of Lossie.* In the fictionalised stories set in the region, Cullen became "Portlossie," Cullen House became "Lossie House," Portknockie became "Scaurnose," and Banff became "Duff Harbour."

During his visits to Cullen, MacDonald preached at the Independent (Congregational) Chapel on Reidhaven Street, and gave several lectures, including one on Robert Burns and another on Tennyson, at the Cullen Town Hall.

MacDonald felt at home with the people of Cullen and Portknockie. As well as visiting in their shops and churches, MacDonald spent much time with local fishermen, listening happily to their tales. The doublet recounting the story of Malcolm's story later secured Cullen's place in the annals of Victorian literature. Both books remain to this day among MacDonald's most beloved works, no less true to this region in which they take place than when first written.

MacDonald's story comes alive to readers when they visit Cullen for the first time. It feels as though they have stepped back in time and are re-living the story through the various scenes MacDonald describes. The Scar Nose, Florimel's Rock (the "Black Fit"), the Bored Craig (also called the Boar Craig and the Bore Craig), the preacher's cave, the clock on the stable wall, the Sea Gate, the Town Gate, and the Grand Entry into Cullen House remain just as they were in MacDonald's time. From Castle Hill one can look down on the Seatown and all the sites mentioned and picture the story unfolding below them.

A Cullen Tour through
Malcolm and *The Marquis of Lossie.*

*Italicized selections from the books are taken
from their new "Cullen Collection" editions.*

From the town square looking west up Grant Street, *Malcolm*
opens in the fictionalised house of Miss Margaret Horn. Her house
occupies a central role throughout the story. We can only
conjecture which of the homes near the square MacDonald
envisioned as that of Miss Horn. Undoubtedly it is that referred to
by J. M. Bulloch in the quote below, where MacDonald is said to
have written some portion of the book and with which he would
have been familiar.

*"The story was largely
written at [—] Grant
Street, Cullen, and
describes that place as
'Portlossie' and Mac-
Donald's great grand-
father's escape from
Culloden...piper, Dun-
can MacPhail...The story
was serialised in the
Glasgow Weekly Herald.
There was a perfect rush on the paper purchasers, I am told by
Mr. Hugh L. Cheyne, who lives in the house where 'Malcolm' was
written, asking not for the Herald, but simply for 'Makim'."* (John
Malcolm Bulloch, *A Centennial Bibliography of George
MacDonald,* Aberdeen, The University Press, 1925, page 29) [1]

---

1 The house number identified in the Bulloch *Bibliography* is withheld, as its
correlation to current numbers cannot be ascertained with positive certainty. It
must also be remembered that today's houses may differ from what they were in
the 1870s, many having undergone both exterior and interior changes since that
time. Identification of the exact house is also complicated by the existence of a
draper's shop at the former site of the Clydesdale Bank building, which stood on
the same side of the street as the even-numbered house identified by Bulloch. For
purposes of the story, MacDonald obviously moved his fictional draper's shop to
the other side of the street so as to be opposite Miss Horn's house.

Duncan Wood explains further: "After the demolition of Cullen's Old Town
and the building of the New Town on a planned grid pattern, many of the first
generation of buildings were of such inferior quality that they showed signs of
decay within only thirty or forty years. Except for the well-built two-story buildings
along Main Street and the Square, most of the rest would have been single-storied.
The expansion of building in Cullen was a slow process that continued as the town
grew. In time many of the original homes from the 1820s and 1830s were
heightened, improved, or demolished and replaced. This was especially true in the
Seatown where in the 1870s-1880s there were many more houses than exist there

The story begins with Miss Horn's neighbour from across the street paying a visit to Miss Horn in the upstairs parlour opposite a room where lay an open coffin.

> *Mrs. Mellis, the wife of the principal draper in the town...had called ostensibly to condole with her, but really to see the corpse. "Indeed, you'll do nothing of the kind! I'll let nobody glower at her that would go and spread such gossip, Mistress Mellis..."*
> *Mrs. Mellis rose in considerable displeasure and with a formal farewell walked from the room, casting a curious glance as she left in the direction of the room in which the body lay.* (*Malcolm*, chapter 1)

After Mrs. Mellis's departure, Miss Horn's privacy is again interrupted by a visit from local midwife Barbara Catanach, who comes in and makes herself at home downstairs in Miss Horn's kitchen.

> *In the kitchen, the floor of which was as white as scrubbing could make it and sprinkled with sea sand...sat a woman of about sixty years of age whose plump pasty face to the first glance looked kindly, to the second, cunning; to the third, evil...She rose as Miss Horn entered, buried a fat fist in her soft side and stood silent.* (*Malcolm*, chapter 1)

A tense visit follows, interrupted by Miss Horn's maid Jean. Miss Horn returns upstairs to her parlour, followed a minute later by Jean, and several minutes after that by Mistress Catanach's departure from the house.

(Much later in the book, as the plot thickens, Miss Horn and Mrs. Mellis will spy on Jean from the Mellis sitting room. The fictionalised Mellis's house would have been upstairs and across the street. Indeed a draper's shop stood at the present site of Bits and Bobs, formerly Clydesdale Bank, for over forty years. [2])

---

today, literally crammed together, many ruinous or with gaping holes and filling every available space. This would have been the Seatown that MacDonald witnessed, far removed from the sanitised version of the Seatown we know today."
2 "The North of Scotland Bank (Clydesdale Bank) building was erected in 1867, replacing a house built originally by local cloth merchant Alexander Lobban in 1821. The present Market Cross was erected in 1872...It incorporates the shaft of the former cross built by local masons...in 1696, and a stone carving of the Town's Arms—the Virgin and Child—of earlier date. Originally the cross stood outside the gates of the Auld Kirk in the middle of the Old Town's main street, but in 1821 it was removed to the top of the Castle Hill, where it remained for about fifty years before being re-erected in the Square. The base of the shaft is still on Castle Hill, together with another old carving from the early cross— 'The King's Arms.' At one time the site proposed for the New Town was about a half mile further south, on the slope overlooking Lintmill." (From Duncan Wood's, *Cullen A Pictorial History*, p. 11.)

Mr. Mellis's shop was directly opposite Miss Horn's house, and his wife's parlour was over the shop, looking into the street…

Mrs. Mellis had so arranged the table and their places, that she and her guest had only to lift their eyes to see the window of their watch. Their plan was, to extinguish their own the moment Jean's light should appear, and so watch without the risk of counter discovery. (Malcolm, chapter 51)

The opening scene continues as Mrs. Catanach turns up the street from Miss Horn's and returns to her own house, presumably at the present intersection of Grant and Castle Streets. Though MacDonald states in a footnote in the book that the story actually takes place fifty years earlier, he clearly uses Cullen of the 1870s as his setting. Which house at this intersection was that of Mrs. Catanach, if any, is a mystery that has been puzzling MacDonald and *Malcolm* aficionados for years.

Before going inside, the midwife paused to gaze down the hill of Castle Street toward the Seatown, harbour, and sea. MacDonald here gives us a panoramic view of his fictional setting of Cullen Bay as it would have been seen in the early 1870s, unobscured by the houses and buildings of today. It must also be remembered that the railway line had not yet been built (which took place in 1886, just a few years after MacDonald's visits), so the viaducts are not mentioned.

When Mistress Catanach arrived at the opening of a street which was just opposite her own door, and led steep toward the sea town, she stood, shaded her eyes with her hooded hand, and although the sun was far behind her, looked out over the sea.

It was the forenoon of a day of early summer. The larks were many and loud in the skies above her—for although she stood in a street, she was only a few yards from the green fields—but she could hardly have heard them. Their music was not for her. To the north across the firth, whither her gaze—if gaze it could be called—was directed, all but cloudless blue heavens stretched over an all but shadowless blue sea. Two bold, jagged promontories, one on each side of her, formed a wide bay. Between that on the west and the sea town at her feet, lay a great curve of yellow sand, upon which the long breakers, born of last night's wind, were still roaring from the northeast. By now, however, the gale had sunk to a breeze—cold and of doubtful influence. From the chimneys of the fishermen's houses in the sea town below ascended a yellowish smoke, which, against the blue of the sea, assumed a dull green colour as it drifted vanishing towards the southwest. (Malcolm, chapter 3)

The description of the landscape continues to the fishing boats which at the time were also gathered on the Cullen side of the bluff of the Scar Nose and Bow Fiddle Rock, before the harbour at Portknockie (fictionalised as "Scaurnose") had been constructed.

Along the shore, in the direction of the great rocky promontory that closed in the bay on the west...

Where the curve of the water line turned northward at the root of the promontory, six or eight fishing boats were drawn up on the beach in various stages of existence. One was little more than half built, the fresh wood shining against the background of dark rock. Another was newly tarred, its sides glistened with the rich shadowy brown, and filled the air with a comfortable odour. Another wore age long neglect on every plank and seam.

Near where they lay, a steep path ascended the cliff. From its top, through grass and ploughed land, the path led across the promontory to the fishing village of Scaurnose, which lay on the other side of it. (*Malcolm*, chapter 3)

MacDonald's brief description of fishermen's wives will ring true even after more than a hundred years for those who remember their own grandmothers selling fish from the creels on their backs.

Their women were often of great strength and courage, and of strongly marked character. They were almost invariably the daughters of fishermen, for a wife taken from among the rural population would have been all but useless for the duties required of her. If these were less dangerous than those of their husbands, they were quite as laborious, and less interesting. The most severe consisted in carrying the fish into the country for sale, in a huge creel or basket, which when full was sometimes more than a man could lift to place on the woman's back.

With this burden, kept in its place by a band across her chest, she would walk as many as twenty miles, arriving at some inland town early in the morning, in time to dispose of her fish for the requirements of the day. (*Malcolm*, chapter 3)

MacDonald's description of the Preacher's Cave extending into the cliffs at the west of the bay will be familiar to residents of Cullen and Portknockie. The cave comes into the story later as the origin of a spiritual revival along the coast.

It was not a very interesting cave to look into. Its strata was upheaved almost to the perpendicular, shaping an opening like the half of a Gothic arch divided vertically and leaning over a little to one side. In length it was only about four or five times its width. The floor was smooth and dry, consisting of hard rock. The walls and roof were jagged with projections and shadowed with recesses, but there was little to rouse any frightful fancies. (*Malcolm*, chapter 3)

Reaching the western end of Cullen Bay, MacDonald shifts his point of view, and describes the coastline as if looking inland from the sea toward the beach, the long dune behind it, the Bored Craig, farmland on the plateau beyond the road, with Cullen Bin in the distance. The imagery—the sweep of Cullen Bay from the harbour to Scar Nose—is as perfectly descriptive today as it was when MacDonald no doubt gazed upon it from Castle Hill.

All the coast to the east of the little harbour was rock, bold and high, of a grey and brown hard stone, which after a mighty sweep, shot out northward, and closed in the bay on that side with a second great promontory. The long curved strip of sand on the west, reaching to the promontory of Scaurnose, was the only open portion of the coast for miles. Here a vessel gliding past the coast gained a pleasant panorama of open fields, belts of wood and farm houses, with now and then a glimpse of a great house amidst its trees. In the distance one or two bare solitary hills, imposing only from their desolation, rose to the height of over a thousand feet.

On this comparatively level part of the shore, parallel with its line and at some distance beyond the usual high water mark, the waves of ten thousand northern storms had cast up a long dune or bank of sand, terminating towards the west within a few yards of a huge red solitary rock of the ugly kind called conglomerate, which must have been separated from the roots of the promontory by the rush of waters at unusually high tides, for in winter they still sometimes rounded the rock, and running down behind the dune, turned it into a long island. The sand on the inland side of the dune was covered with short sweet grass and the largest and reddest of daisies,

*and was browsed on by sheep. It was also occasionally swept by
wild salt waves, and when the northern wind blew straight as
an arrow and keen as a sword from the regions of endless snow,
lay under a sheet of gleaming ice.* (*Malcolm*, chapter 4)

At last we meet Malcolm himself, walking along the dune,
with the sound of bagpipes drifting over the morning air behind
him from the town's piper, his own blind grandfather, whose duty
it was each morning to rouse the sleepers of Portlossie to the new
day. This Duncan MacPhail is one of the most colourful and
memorable characters in MacDonald's rich corpus of personalities,
and was drawn from MacDonald's own great-grandfather, the
blind piper of Portsoy.

*The sun had been up
for some time in a
cloudless sky. The wind
had changed to the
south, and wafted soft
country odours to the
shore, in place of
sweeping to inland farms
the scents of seaweed and
broken salt waters,
mingled with a suspicion
of icebergs. From what
was called the Seaton, or
seatown, of Portlossie, a
crowd of cottages occupied entirely by fisher-folk, a solitary
figure was walking westward along this grass at the back of the
dune, singing. On his left hand the ground rose to the high road.
On his right was the dune, interlaced and bound together by the
long clasping roots of the coarse grass, without which its sands
would have been but the sport of every wind that blew. It shut
out from him all sight of the sea, but the moan and rush of the*

rising tide sounded close behind it. At his back rose the town of Portlossie, high above the harbour and the Seaton, with its houses of grey and brown stone, roofed with blue slates and red tiles. It was no highland town—almost no one in it could speak the highland tongue. Yet down from its high streets on the fitful air of the morning now floated intermittently the sound of bagpipes—borne winding from street to street, and loud blown to wake the sleeping inhabitants and let them know that it was now six o'clock.

The young man on the dune was a youth of about twenty, with a long, swinging, heavy footed stride, which took in the ground rapidly—a movement unlike that of the other men of the place, who always walked slowly, and never but on dire compulsion ran. He was tall and large limbed. His dress was like that of a fisherman, consisting of blue serge trowsers, a shirt striped blue and white, and a Guernsey frock, which he carried flung across his shoulder. On his head he wore a round blue bonnet, with a tuft of scarlet in the centre. (*Malcolm*, chapter 4)

Malcolm completes his portion of the daily ritual to accompany his grandfather's bagpipes. At precisely the hour of six o'clock, he sets off the town cannon.

About the middle of the long sandhill, a sort of wide opening was cut in its top, in which stood an old-fashioned brass swivel-gun. When the lad reached the place, he sprang up the sloping side of the dune, seated himself on the gun, drew from his trowsers a large silver watch, regarded it steadily for a few minutes, replaced it, took from his pocket a flint and steel with which he kindled a bit of touch-paper which he applied to the vent of the swivel. A great roar followed. (*Malcolm*, chapter 4)

We now meet Lady Florimel, daughter of the Marquis of Lossie. Up early with the northern summer sunrise, she has been reading while sitting on one of a small group of rocks known as "the Black Fit" (or *Foot*). Startled by the explosion from the cannon, she suddenly realizes that she has been stranded by the incoming tide. Her unceremonious rescue by Malcolm sets in motion a tempestuous relationship between the prim and proper "lady" and the presumptuous, plain-spoken, humble fisherman.

Its echoes had nearly died away when a startled little cry reached his ears. Looking to the shore, he discovered a young woman on a low rock that ran a

little way out into the water. She had half risen from a sitting posture and had apparently just discovered that the rising tide had surrounded her. There was no danger whatever, but the girl might well shrink from plunging into the clear depth of a foot or two in which swayed the seaweed covering the slippery slopes of the rock.

He rushed from the sandhill, crying out as he approached her, "Dinna move, mem! Stay where ye are till I get to ye."

He ran straight into the water and struggled through the deepening tide—the distance being short and the depth too shallow for swimming. In a moment he was by her side, scarcely saw the bare feet she had been bathing in the water, and heeded as little the motion of her hand which waved him back. He caught her in his arms like a baby and had her safe on the shore before she could utter a word. Nor did he stop until he had carried her to the slope of the sandhill where he set her down gently without the least suspicion of the liberty he was taking and filled only with a passion of service. He proceeded to dry her feet with the frock he had dropped there as he ran to her assistance. (*Malcolm*, chapter 4)

Returning across the burn, visitors who have tried to find a pattern to its cottages, streets, and lanes will smile at MacDonald's description of the Seatown.

The sea town of Portlossie was as irregular a gathering of small cottages as could be found on the surface of the globe. They faced every way, and turned their backs and gables in every direction. Only of the roofs could you predict the position. They were divided from each other by every sort of small, irregular space and passage, and looked like a national assembly debating a constitution. Close behind the Seaton ran a highway, climbing far above the chimneys of the village to the level of the town above. Behind this road, and separated from it by a high wall of stone, lay a succession of heights and hollows covered with grass. In front of the cottages lay sand and sea. The place was cleaner than most fishing villages, but so closely built, so thickly inhabited, and so pervaded with "a very ancient and fishlike smell," that but for the broom of the salt north wind it must have been unhealthy. Eastward the houses could extend no further for

the harbour, and westward no further for a small river that crossed the sands to find the sea—discursively and merrily at low water, but with sullen, submissive mingling when banked back by the tide. (Malcolm, chapter 5)

In the Seatown we meet Malcolm's colourful grandfather Duncan in person, encountering again the Doric which characterizes much of the book's dialogue, as well as the peculiar use of feminine articles and characteristic Highland flavour of the dialect when it rolls off Duncan's tongue.

Avoiding the many nets extended long and wide on the grassy sands, the youth walked through the tide-swollen mouth of the river, and passed along the front of the village until he arrived at a house, the small window in the seaward gable of which was filled with a curious collection of things for sale— dusty looking sweets in a glass bottle, gingerbread cakes in the shape of large hearts, thickly studded with sugar plums of rainbow colours, strings of tin covers for tobacco-pipes overlapping each other like fish scales, toys, and tapes, and needles, and twenty other kinds of things, all huddled together.

Turning the corner of this house, he went down the narrow passage between it and the next, and in at its open door. But the moment it was entered it lost all appearance of a shop, and the room with the tempting window showed itself only as a poor kitchen with an earthen floor.

"Weel, hoo did the pipes behave themselves today, daddy?" he said as he strode in.

"Och, she was a good poy today," returned the tremulous voice of a gray-haired old man who was leaning over a small peat-fire on the hearth, sifting oatmeal through the fingers of his left hand while he stirred the boiling mess with a short stick held in his right. (Malcolm, chapter 5)

A little later Malcolm walks up from the Seatown into the upper town on his way through the fields to the Auld Kirk and the former Old Town of Portlossie. The view across the Moray Firth to Sutherland is one that will be familiar to all.

As soon as his grandfather left the house, Malcolm went out also, closing the door behind him and turning the key but leaving it in the lock. He ascended to the upper town and turned to look back for a few moments. The descent to the shore was so sudden that he could see nothing of the harbour or the village he had left—nothing but the blue bay before him and the filmy mountains of Sutherlandshire in the distance to the left as the coastline gradually swung around northward. After gazing for a moment he turned and continued on his way, through Portlossie and out beyond through the fields.

The morning was glorious, the larks jubilant, and the air filled with the sweet scents of cottage flowers. Across the fields came the occasional low of an ox and the distant sounds of children at play.

(*Malcolm*, chapter 6)

A few days later we encounter Malcolm walking through the town, selling his catch of fish as he makes his way to Lossie House, where he supplies fish to the housekeeper. He encounters Mistress Catanach a short way down from the "Town Gate" at the top of Grant Street.

Malcolm walked up through the town with his fish, hoping to part with some of the less desirable of them and so lighten his basket before entering the grounds of Lossie House. But he had met with little success and was now approaching the town gate, as they called it, which closed a short street at right angles to the principal one, when he came upon Mrs. Catanach—on her knees cleaning her doorstep. (*Malcolm*, chapter 8)

As Malcolm continues, the entry into Lossie House appears exactly as it does as we walk into the grounds today.

By a winding carriage drive, through trees whose growth was stunted by the sea winds, Malcolm made a slow descent, yet was soon shadowed by timber of a more prosperous growth, rising as from a lake of the loveliest green, spangled with starry daisies. The air was full of sweet odours uplifted with the ascending dew, and trembled with a hundred songs at once, for here was a very paradise for birds.

*At length he came in sight of a long low wing of the house, and
went to the door that led to the kitchen.* (*Malcolm*, chapter 8)

The first sight of habitation the visitor of today to the estate
encounters is the expansive white residence of the Earl of Seafield,
formerly the factor's house. In a simple description to open the
second book of his doublet, MacDonald colourfully describes the
stable yard and clock, which can still be seen above what are today
the garages of the Earl.

*It was one of those exquisite days that come in every winter,
in which it seems no longer the dead body, but the lovely ghost
of summer. Such a day bears to its sister of the happier time
something of the relation the marble statue bears to the living
form. It lifts the soul into a higher region than will summer day
of lordliest splendour. It is like the love that loss has purified.*

*Such, however, were not the thoughts that at the moment
occupied the mind of Malcolm Colonsay. Indeed, the loveliness
of the morning was but partially visible from the spot where he*

*stood—the stable yard of Lossie
House, ancient and roughly
paved. It was a hundred years
since the stones had been last
relaid and levelled. None of the
horses of the late Marquis
minded it but one—her whom
the young man in Highland
dress was now grooming—and
she would have fidgeted had it
been an oak floor. The yard was
a long and wide space, with two-storied buildings on all sides of
it. In the centre of one of them rose the clock, and the morning
sun shone red on its tarnished gold. It was an ancient clock, but
still capable of keeping good time—good enough, at least, for all
the requirements of the house, even when the family was at
home, seeing it never stopped, and the church clock was always
ordered by it.*

*It not only set the time, but seemed also to set the fashion of
the place, for the whole aspect of it was one of wholesome,
weather beaten, time-worn existence. One of the good things that
accompany good blood is that its possessor does not much mind
a shabby coat. Tarnish and lichens and water-wearing, a wavy
house-ridge, and a few families of worms in the wainscot do not
annoy the marquis as they do the city man who has just bought
a little place in the country. An old tree is venerable, and an old
picture precious to the soul, but an old house, on which has been
laid none but loving and respectful hands, is dear to the very
heart. Even an old barn door, with the carved initials of hinds and
maidens of vanished centuries, has a place of honour in the
cabinet of the poet's brain. It was centuries since Lossie House*

11

had begun to grow shabby—and beautiful. And he to whom it now belonged was not one to let the vanity of possession interfere with the grandeur of inheritance. (The Marquis of Lossie, chapter 1)

Continuing past the factor's home, Malcolm at length arrives at Lossie House, which is destined to play such a central role in the ongoing story. His description of the House, the bridge, the burn, and the expansive grounds spreading inland all the way to Cullen Bin are timeless, and no less descriptive of the majesty of Cullen House today than they were almost a century and a half ago.

The house was an ancient pile, mainly of two sides at right angles, but with many gables, mostly having corbel steps—a genuine old Scottish dwelling, small windowed and gray, with steep slated roofs, and many turrets, each with a conical top. Some of these turrets rose from the ground, encasing spiral stone stairs. Others were but bartizans, their interiors forming recesses in rooms. They gave the house something of the air of a French chateau, only it looked stronger and far grimmer. Carved around some of the windows, in ancient characters, were Scripture texts and antique proverbs. Two time worn specimens of heraldic zoology, in a state of fearful and everlasting excitement, stood rampant and gaping, one on each side of the hall door, contrasting strangely with the repose of the ancient house, which looked very like what the oldest part of it was said to have been— a monastery. It had at the same time, however, a somewhat warlike expression, though it could never have been capable of much defence, although its position in that regard was splendid.

In front was a great gravel space, in the centre of which lay a huge block of serpentine, from a quarry on the estate, as a pivot around which the carriages turned.

On one side of the house was a great stone bridge, of lofty span, stretching across a little glen, in which ran a brown stream spotted with foam—the same that entered the firth beside the Seaton. It was not muddy, however, for though dark it was clear—its brown being a rich transparent hue, almost red, gathered from the peat bogs of the great moorland hill behind. Only a very narrow terrace walk, with battlemented parapet, lay between the back of the house, and a precipitous descent of a hundred feet to this rivulet. Up its banks, lovely with flowers and rich with shrubs and trees below, you might ascend until by slow gradations you left the woods and all culture behind, and found yourself, though still within the precincts of Lossie House, on the lonely side of the waste hill, a thousand feet above the sea.

The hall door stood open...This portion of the building was so narrow that the hall occupied its entire width, and on the opposite side of it another door, standing also open, gave a glimpse of the glen.

(*Malcolm*, chapter 8)

Thus concludes MacDonald's initial tour of the bay, the Seatown, the upper town, and the grounds of Lossie House. As *Malcolm* proceeds, however, the portrayals of Cullen and its environs continue to infuse the story with a delicious sense of reality—some mere snatches, others lengthy descriptions easily recognised. No book of MacDonald's is so true to place as *Malcolm's* depiction of Cullen and its surroundings.

Anyone familiar with the northeast of Scotland will recognise the weather described by MacDonald.

That night the weather changed and grew cloudy and cold. A northeast wind tore off the tops of the drearily tossing billows. All was gray—enduring, hopeless gray. Along the coast the waves kept roaring on the sands, persistent and fateful. The Scaurnose was one mass of foaming white, and in the caves still

haunted by the tide, the bellowing was like that of thunder.
(*Malcolm,* chapter 9)

MacDonald likewise brings the fishing life alive that dominated Scotland's north coast for most of the 19ᵗʰ century.

> *Nor did Portlossie alone send out her boats, like huge seabirds warring on the live treasures of the deep. From beyond the headlands east and west, out they glided on slow red wing, from Scaurnose, from Sandend, from Clamrock, from the villages all along the coast—spreading as they came, each to its work apart through all the laborious night, to rejoin its fellows only as home drew them back in the clear gray morning, laden and slow with the harvest of the stars. But the night lay between, into which they were sailing over waters of heaving green that for ever kept tossing up roses—a night whose curtain was a horizon built up of steady blue, but gorgeous with passing purple and crimson, and flashing with molten gold. (Malcolm, chapter 21)*

A great outdoor feast given by the Marquis for the neighbourhood gives another look at the grounds and the several entrances to Cullen House.

> *A bridge of stately span, level with the sweep in front, honourable embodiment of the savings of a certain notable countess, one end resting on the same rock with the house, their foundations almost in contact, led across the burn to more and more trees, their roots swathed in the finest grass, through which ran broad carriage drives and narrower footways, hard and smooth with yellow gravel. Here amongst the trees were set long tables for the fishermen, mechanics, and farm labourers. Here also was the place appointed for the piper.*

14

As the hour drew near, the guests came trooping in at every entrance. By the sea gate came the fisher folk, many of the men in the blue jersey, the women mostly in short print gowns of large patterns. Each group that entered had a joke or jibe for Johnny Bykes, which he met in varying but always surly fashion. By the town gate came the people of Portlossie. By the new main entrance from the high road beyond the town, through lofty Greekish gates, came the lords and lairds, in yellow coaches, gigs and post-chaises. By another gate, far up the glen, came most of the country folk, some walking, some riding, all merry and with the best of intentions of enjoying themselves. As

the common people approached the house, they were directed to their different tables by the sexton, for he knew everybody.

The marquis was early on the ground, going about amongst his guests and showing a friendly off-hand courtesy which influenced everyone favourably toward him. Lady Florimel soon joined him, and a certain frank way she inherited from her father, joined to the great beauty her mother had given her, straightway won all hearts. (*Malcolm*, chapter 22)

The tunnel from the beach to the temple, now closed off, is the scene of a violent storm which traps Malcolm and Florimel in its downpour. Knowing of the tunnel, Florimel leads Malcolm through it, and then in safety back to Lossie House.

Suddenly came a great blinding flash and a roar through the leaden air, followed by heavy drops mixed with hailstones.

At the flash, Florimel gave a cry and half rose to her feet, but at the thunder, she fell as if stunned by the noise. With a bound Malcolm was by her side, but when she perceived his terror for her, she smiled and, laying hold of his hand, sprang to her feet.

"Come, come," she cried, and, still holding his hand, hurried up the dune and down the other side of it. Malcolm accompanied her step for step, strongly tempted, however, to snatch her up and run for the bored craig which would offer them the most ready protection. He could not think why she made for the road—high on an unscalable embankment, with the park wall on the other side. But she ran straight for a door in the embankment itself, dark between two buttresses, which having never seen it open, he had not thought of.

She stood panting, while with trembling hand she put a key in the lock. The next moment she pushed open the creaking door and entered. As she turned to take out the key, she saw Malcolm yards away in a cataract of rain. He stood with his hat in his hand, watching for a farewell glance.

"Why don't you come in?" she said impatiently.

He was beside her in a moment.

"I didna ken ye wanted me in," he said.

"I wouldn't have you drowned," she returned, shutting the door.

"Drowned!" he repeated. "It would take a great deal to drown me. I stuck to the bottom of an overturned boat a whole night when I was but fifteen."

They stood in a tunnel which passed under the road, affording immediate communication between the park grounds of Lossie House and the shore. ...

They walked through and left the far end of the tunnel. Skirting the bottom of a little hill, they were presently in the midst of a young wood through which a gravelled path led toward the House. (*Malcolm*, chapter 15)

The following morning Malcolm has one of several encounters with one Johnny Bykes, keeper of the "Sea Gate" to the grounds of Lossie House. This is the third of four entrances to the grounds and often the first seen by present day visitors to Cullen, standing as it does directly under the stone viaduct where Cullen Burn spills out across the sands and into the sea.

With eyes intent and keen as those of a gaze-hound, Malcolm retraced every step up to the tunnel. But no volume was to be seen. Turning from the door, for which he had no key, he climbed to the foot of the wall that crossed it above, and with a bound, a clutch at the top, and a pull and a scramble, was on the high road in a moment. From the road he dropped on the other side to the grass where, from the grated door on the beach side, he retraced their path from the dune. Lady Florimel had dropped the book when she rose from the sand, and there Malcolm found it. He wrapped it in its owner's handkerchief and set out for the gate at the mouth of the river.

As he came to the gate onto the precincts of Lossie House, the keeper, a snarling fellow by the name of Bykes who was overly taken with his mediocre authority, rushed out of the lodge and, just as Malcolm was entering, shoved the gate in his face.

"You won't come in without my leave," he cried with a vengeful expression.

"What's that for?" said Malcolm, who had already interposed his great boot so that the spring bolt could not reach its catch.

"There's no land-jumping rascals come in here," said Bykes setting his shoulder to the gate.

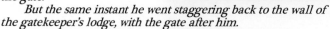

But the same instant he went staggering back to the wall of the gatekeeper's lodge, with the gate after him.

"Stick to the wall there," said Malcolm as he strode in.

The keeper pursued him with frantic abuse, but Malcolm never turned his head. (*Malcolm*, chapter 15)

An outing and picnic at Findlater Castle, fictionalised as "Colonsay Castle," nearly has disastrous consequences.

Here low rocks, infinitely broken and jagged, filled all the tidal space. High cliffs of gray and brown rock, orange and green with lichen here and there, and in summer crowned with golden gorse, rose behind—untouched by the ordinary tide, but at high water lashed by the waves of a storm.

Beyond the headland which they were fast nearing, the cliffs and the sea met at half-tide.

The moment they rounded it—

"Look there, my lord," cried Malcolm, *"there's Colonsay Castle, that yer lordship gets your name frae. It must be many a hundred years since any Colonsay lived in it!"*

Well he might say so, for they looked but saw nothing—only cliff beyond cliff rising from a white-fringed shore. Not a broken tower, not a ragged battlement invaded the horizon.

"There's nothing of the sort there!" said Lady Florimel.

"You mustna look for a tower or pinnacle, my leddy, for ye winna see any. Their time's long over. But jist get the face of the cliffs in yer eye, and travel along it until ye come to a place that looks like mason work. It hardly rises above the cliff in most places, but here and there is a few feet of it."

Following his direction, Lady Florimel soon found the ruin. The front of a projecting portion of the cliff was faced with mason work, while on its side, the masonry rested upon jutting

masses of the rock. Above, grass-grown heaps and mounds, and one isolated bit of wall pierced with a little window, like an empty eye-socket with no skull behind it, was all that was visible from the sea of the structure which had once risen lordly on the crest of the cliff.

"It is poor for a ruin even!" said Lord Lossie...

Almost immediately followed a slight grating noise, which grew loud, and before one could say her speed had slackened, the cutter rested on the pebbles, with the small waves of the just-turned tide flowing against her quarter. Malcolm was overboard in a moment...

They were in a little valley, open only to the sea, one boundary of which was the small promontory on which the castle stood. The side of it next to them rose perpendicular from the beach to a great height. From there, to gain the summit, they had to ascend by a winding path till they reached the approach to the castle from the landward side....

They set out to have a peep at the ruins and choose a place for luncheon.

From the point where they stood, looking seaward, the ground sank to the narrow isthmus supposed by Malcolm to fill a cleft formerly crossed by a drawbridge and, beyond it, rose again to the grassy mounds in which lay so many of the old bones of the ruined carcass. Passing along the isthmus, where one side was the little bay in which they had landed, they clambered up a rude ascent of solid rock, and so reached what had been the centre of the seaward portion of the castle.

Here they came suddenly upon a small hole at their feet, going right down. Florimel knelt and, looking in, saw the remains of a small spiral stair. The opening seemed large enough to let her through. She gathered her garments tight *about her, and was halfway buried in the earth before her father, whose attention had been drawn elsewhere, saw what she was about…*

At length Florimel found herself on the upper end of a steep sloping ridge of hard, smooth earth, lying along the side of one chamber and leading across to yet another beyond, which, unlike the rest, was full of light. The passion of exploration being by this time thoroughly roused in her, she descended the slope, half sliding, half creeping.

When she thus reached the hole into the bright chamber, she almost sickened with horror. The slope went off steeper, till it rushed, as it were, out of a huge gap in the wall of the castle, laying bare the void of space and the gleam of the sea at a frightful depth below. If she had gone one foot farther, she could not have saved herself from sliding out of the gap.

She gave a shriek of terror, and grabbed hold of the broken wall. To heighten her dismay she found at the very first effort, partly, no doubt, from the paralysis of fear, that it was impossible to climb back up. There she lay on the verge of the steeper slope, her head and shoulders in the inner of the two chambers, and the rest of her body in the outer, with the hideous vacancy staring at her. In a few moments it had fascinated her so that she dared not close her eyes lest it should leap upon her. The wonder was that she did not lose her consciousness and fall at once to the bottom of the cliff. (Malcolm, chapters 36-37)

MacDonald's description of the old Cullen Kirk is not only picturesque, it gives a precise and wonderful visual image of the church as it still stands today.

It was a cruciform building, as old as the vanished monastery, and the burial place of generations of noble blood. The dust of royalty even lay under its floor. A knight of stone reclined cross legged in a niche with an arched Norman canopy in one of the walls, the rest of which was nearly encased in large tablets of white marble, for at his foot lay the ashes of barons and earls whose title was extinct, and whose lands had been inherited by the family of Lossie. Inside as well as outside of the church the ground had risen with the dust of generations, so that the walls were low, and heavy

galleries having been erected in parts, the place was filled with shadowy recesses and haunted with glooms. (*Malcolm*, chapter 10)

Banff, too, comes in for its share of the story, fictionalised as "Duff Harbour." The story's "Fife House" represents Banff's Duff House, which has beautiful grounds open to the public.

At length the coach drove into the town, and stopped at the Duff Arms. Miss Horn descended, straightened her long back with some difficulty, shook her feet, loosened her knees, and after a tip to the guard more liberal than was customary, in acknowledgment of the kindness she had been unable to accept, marched off with the stride of a grenadier to find her lawyer.

Their interview did not relieve her of much of the time, which now hung upon her like a cloak of lead, and the earliness of the hour would not have deterred her from at once commencing a round of visits to the friends she had in the place. But the gates of the lovely environs of Fife House stood open, and although there were no flowers now, and the trees were leafless, waiting in poverty and patience for their coming riches, they drew her with the offer of a plentiful loneliness and room. She accepted it, entered, and for two hours wandered about their woods and walks.

By and by she came out of the woods, and found herself on the banks of the Wan Water, a broad, fine river, here talking in wide rippled innocence from bank to bank, there lying silent and motionless and gloomy, as if all the secrets of the drowned since the creation of the world lay dim floating in its shadowy bosom. In great sweeps it sought the ocean, and the trees stood back from its borders, leaving a broad margin of grass between, as if the better to see it go. Just outside the grounds and before reaching the sea, it passed under a long bridge of many arches— then, trees and grass and flowers and all greenery left behind, rushed through a waste of storm-heaped pebbles into the world-water. Miss Horn followed it out of the grounds and on to the beach.

Here its channel was constantly changing. Even while she stood gazing at its rapid rush, its bank of pebbles and sand fell almost from under her feet. But her thoughts were so busy that she scarcely observed even what she saw, and hence it was not strange that she should be unaware of having been followed and watched all the way. Now from behind a tree, now from a corner of the mausoleum, now from behind a rock, now over the parapet of the bridge, the mad laird had watched her. From a heap of rock on the opposite side of the Wan Water, he was watching her now. Again and again he had made a sudden movement as if to run and accost her, but had always drawn back again and concealed himself more carefully than before.

At length she turned in the direction of the town. It was a quaint old place—a royal burgh for five centuries, with streets irregular and houses of much individuality. Most of the latter

were humble in appearance, bare and hard in form, and gray in hue. But there were curious corners, low archways, uncompromising gables, some with corbel steps— now and then an outside stair, a delicious little dormer window, or a gothic doorway, sometimes with a bit of carving over it. [3]

With the bent head of the climber, Miss Horn was walking up a certain street, called from its precipitousness the Strait, that is difficult, Path—an absolute Hill of Difficulty, when she was accosted by an elderly man, who stood in the doorway of one of the houses. (*Malcolm*, chapter 53)

This has been but a quick "tour" through the story—a mere taste of *many* vivid descriptions in the books themselves. They truly provide "a Victorian literary portrait of Cullen." What could be more enjoyable now than to take the brief walk up to Castle Hill 200 yards in through the Town Gate. From this spectacular vantage point, you will be able to scan the entire panorama of the walking tour we have just taken through the books. The view stretches from Lossiemouth to the west (whose name MacDonald borrowed for his story) to Troup Head eastward (whose namesake descendants are intimately intertwined with MacDonald's personal history and was a site also visited by MacDonald).

---

3 *Miss Horn's destination is the fictional town of "Duff Harbour," a representation of the neighbouring town of Banff, approximately thirteen miles east along the coast from Cullen, Banff being the ancient county seat of Banffshire. MacDonald's description here corresponds wonderfully with Banff, as Miss Horn walks about the grounds of "Fife House" (Duff House), to the mouth of the Deveron River (which here, as in Alec Forbes of Howglen, MacDonald fictionalises into the Wan Water), through the town and up the exceedingly steep "Strait" path. As with Cullen/Portlossie, his description precisely reflects the reality of the place. The beach at the mouth of the Devoron is special to us as the first place we saw dolphins in Scotland, and we usually visit Banff once or twice every summer.—MP*

Contemporary Letters and Accounts of George MacDonald's Visits to Cullen

The visit of 1872

In the late spring of 1872, George and Louisa MacDonald took the train north to Scotland lecturing in several cities on their way, including a lecture on Tennyson in Edinburgh. Though they planned to visit MacDonald's home town of Huntly, the main purpose of the trip was a visit to Cullen in preparation for MacDonald's new book.

Arriving in Cullen in late April of 1872, George and Louisa stayed at the Seafield Arms Hotel, the "inn" Louisa refers to, but also spent time at Cullen House—whether lodging there (doubtful) or only visiting during the day (probable) is unknown. The Countess of Seafield was away but apparently left them a key. They also spent time with Rev. Ker and his wife at the manse of the Deskford Free Church inland from Cullen about five miles. Beyond that, Louisa's letters to her children back home in the south of England are vague about the specifics of their movements and lodgings. Their stay in Deskford particularly intrigues me as I suspect Deskford (also known as "Kirktown of Deskford") to be the name upon which MacDonald drew for his fictional Kirkbyres in the novel. (The moor MacDonald describes on the way to Kirkbyres, however, is a few miles *beyond* Deskford, making the distance from Cullen to Deskford considerably shorter than from Portlossie to Kirkbyres in the book.)

One thing Louisa's letters are *not* vague about—how much her husband loved Cullen and felt at home among its people. In another interesting detail, in the book MacDonald speaks of the pleasant aroma coming from the saddler's shop, mentioned by Louisa outside their hotel window. Strachan's saddlery (pictured) was one of Cullen's longest standing 19th century businesses.

Letters from Seafield Arms Hotel from Louisa MacDonald

Seafield Arms Hotel,
Monday April 29.
This is a nice interesting place. It is not so cold as I expected. I sat on a rock for a whole hour today waiting for Papa who went on farther than I would go—and I really enjoyed the air very much. The sea is so divinely clear—the grass grows down to the water's edge—& the sands are very nice to walk on. The fishing village roofs are picturesque—thatched and red tiles—but I can't

say further than that—but then I am not Scotch you see & it takes a long time to see these things as having any comfort in them.
We are in a nice enough Inn, and I hope we shall be able to remain here, though we have no prospect from our windows but some small houses—one of which has over the door Mr. Strachan, Saddler.
Papa is so well—I am sure he is enjoying all the Scotch surroundings exceedingly—tho' he is getting a little anxious about his new book wh. is not yet begun. He thought we were so lucky in having got to a place where we shd. not have to speak at all unless we liked as we don't mind being silent to each

other—but while we were sitting at tea—the first evening…in walked a young lady who declared she couldn't find George MacDonald the author's house, and had come to see him. She told us how all the town knew we were here—comforting assurance!…The Countess of Seafield…is just gone to London— so we shall not see her—but Papa has written to her to ask her for the run of her house. The estate is very fine—including woods—wh. however I have only seen at a distance—the rest of the country is bare just here—but we had a lovely walk yesterday morning Papa & I—we heard the larks singing over the sea, & over the cornfields. We like being out so much—so different from our last year in Holland.—Mr. & Mrs. Ker…came here this morning to invite us to their house—to stay a day or two—we are going to spend Saturday there—he is a Brd. Church minister…& seems a pleasant gentleman. [4]

A few days later, referencing their visit to Deskford, Louisa writes:

Cullen.
Saturday.
We got your telegram at Deskford the free kirk manse. The Kers. Such a sweet family…
The quiet here— is something to be real thankful for. Papa seems so quietly happy. He enjoys going out so much & loves talking to all the fisher people and country folk & they really are so nice, though not nearly so pleasant or polite as the Highlanders. We have made arrangements today to stay here a fortnight, so I have no bother with housekeeping— wh. I fancy would be a problem as there are no shops to speak of & I should not know how to find out where to get sugar and meat. The house is very comfortable & the people amusing & kind…
I dare say I shall come to you—next week at any rate. Papa is going to lecture in Dundee, Liverpool & Leicester going back—but he won't mind my going to you & I should not think of your having everything to do without me. [5]

Whether her reference to staying on another two weeks meant at the manse in Deskford or in Cullen itself, it is difficult to know. It hardly seems she would have been concerned about provisions in either place, either as guests of the Kers, or in town. Indeed, Cullen had a profusion of shops of every kind.

4 Letter home from Louisa, April 29, 1872, sent from the Seafield Arms Hotel, quoted in *Wingfold* #99, Summer 2017, and in *George MacDonald Victorian Mythmaker,* Rolland Hein, p. 234.
5 Letter home from Louisa, May 4, 1872, quoted in *Wingfold* #99 Summer 2017, p. 38.

In any event, two days later, they *had* returned the five miles to Cullen, when the following letter was written. MacDonald had apparently thought of renting a fisherman's cottage, but they were again at the hotel on the high street, now the A98 through town. Louisa's letter is headed with the words, "Seafield Arms Hotel," though the reference to staying in a "house" adds another small puzzle to the sequence of their movements and lodgings. By the "landlady" of the "house," she clearly means the proprietress of the Seafield Arms Hotel. The *landlady* of the fictional Lossie Arms is twice referenced in the story, including, in Chapter 22, her skill at cooking for large groups, which Louisa also mentions. Louisa writes:

SEAFIELD ARMS HOTEL

> Seafield Arms Hotel,
> Cullen, Banffshire,
> Monday.
> Very glad to have had your letter from home…
> This is a nice place—nice sky, lovely cream, plenty of salt fish, beautiful sea, lovely cakes, scones, & biscuits—respectable mutton—fine rocks—lots of poor fishermen's houses—think Papa has changed his mind about living in one of them. It isn't Devonshire & one has to learn the cold bare bleakness before one can admire it. People all nice & friendly. Landlady a character, jolly woman—cooked for a regiment mess for fifteen years before she & her husband took this house. Told Papa yesterday he needs not think to pass anywhere without being known. 'Some people have to wait till they die to be known & be talked about—but that's not your case Sir'…
> Papa does enjoy this place so much. [6]

Rolland Hein notes:

"He and Louisa thought they would unobtrusively spend a quiet time, uninterrupted by people. The keeper of the hotel told

---

6 Letter home from Louisa, May 6, 1872, from the "Seafield Arms Hotel, Cullen, Banffshire, Monday," quoted in *Wingfold* #99 Summer 2017, pp. 38-39.

them on arriving, however, that they need not think to pass anywhere unrecognised. Finding themselves beset with local fans, they managed hastily to secure the nearby estate of the Countess of Seafield, who was visiting in London at the time, for the weeks they spent in Cullen." [7]

During their visit, MacDonald was informed that the Cullen library and newsroom were in need of financial assistance. He offered to give a lecture on "The Lyrics of Tennyson," the same lecture he had delivered in Edinburgh on his way north, with the proceeds going to the library. He gave the lecture at the Cullen Town Hall, and also preached at the Congregational Church.

From the *Banffshire Journal* about MacDonald's Tennyson lecture

"Dr. and Mrs. George MacDonald have been on a visit to Cullen during the past fortnight. The fact that the library and news-room of the town were in need of aid having been brought under Dr. MacDonald's notice, he consented to deliver a lecture in aid of the institution." [8]

From the *Elgin Courant*

"It is needless to say that the lecture was a masterpiece." [9]

On Sunday May 12, 1872, MacDonald preached in the Cullen Congregational Chapel.

---

7 *George MacDonald, Victorian Mythmaker,* Rolland Hein, p. 234. The fascinating piece of information that the MacDonalds stayed at Cullen House is unconfirmed and *may* be inaccurate. A letter from their visit the following year indicates that they visited the house and grounds of Cullen House in 1873, but there is no evidence to confirm that they actually *lodged* at Cullen House on either visit.

8 The *Banffshire Journal*, May 14, 1872, quoted in *Wingfold* #80, p. 6.

9 The *Elgin Courant*, May 10, 1872, quoted in *Wingfold* #80, p. 6.

From the *Banffshire Journal*
> "A more graphic and faithful sermon, and impressive service throughout, all who were present—and the house was full—admit there scarcely could have been."[10]

After their visit to Cullen, Louisa returned to London while MacDonald himself continued south more slowly, lecturing on the way as Louisa had mentioned in her letter above. The letter from Liverpool I find interesting simply from the touching personal exchange with Louisa—he seems so innocently childlike when writing to her!—and also from the fact that he is still struggling to finish *The Vicar's Daughter* proofs.

Letters home from George MacDonald

> *Huntly*
> *May 20, 1872*
> *I must try to work on my proofs in the trains, or I don't know how I shall get through with the last of the Vicar which is now being lugged from me. I am going to preach here tomorrow evening. The sun is just breaking out of the stormy clouds in the west and shining through a thin falling snow.* [11]

> *Richmond Park May 24, 1872,*
> *[Liverpool]*
> *You won't mind a short note, dearest—for I have been busy with the Vicar's Daughter all day, & now I must see to my lecture this evening for I am far from ready. Thanks many for your letters. It was very stupid of me to forget last night to write to you. I meant to do it of course, but was very tired, & it went out of my head. I have this morning had the nice long letter you sent to the Cupples. The Postmaster sent it on here.*
> *I made Noble take £5 for his work—that leaves me £14 for last night...Maurice and I leave about one tomorrow for Leicester...*
> *I long to be home to you, darling. I am dull & stupid, but able to work, & have nothing particular the matter. I sent you a telegram this morning, & here is a cheque for £10...I feel restless till I get home. My love to all the creatures.*
>
> > *Dear love,*
> > *Your Husband.* [12]

---

10 The *Banffshire Journal*, May 21, 1872, quoted in *Wingfold* #80, p. 6.

11 Letter from Huntly: George MacDonald to Louisa, who had then returned to England, May 20, 1872, from *George MacDonald and His Wife* by Greville MacDonald, p. 418.

12 GMD to Louisa, May 24, 1872, *Wingfold* #99, Summer 2017, p. 48.

About his several encounters with MacDonald during that spring of 1872, the reminiscences of a certain W. McK Bell were printed forty years later in an English newspaper (1912, in the *Shields Daily News*). We love this account as the "Salmon Bothy loop" is one of Judy's favourite walks when we are in Cullen, another example how *alive* Mac-Donald's visits to Cullen remain even after all these years.

Mr. Bell said his first acquaintance with...Dr. Geo. MacDonald took place in his native village on the shores of the Moray Firth, in Banffshire. It occurred in a rather unusual place, a salmon fisherman's bothy. The doctor was fond of strolling about the lovely little bays backed by high precipitous cliffs that are such a delightful characteristic of the Moray Firth coast, and generally called in at the fisherman's bothy. Nothing delighted him better than to have a 'crack' with these hardy sun-browned toilers of the deep.

The novelist was residing in this remote Banffshire village for the purpose of writing his novels entitled 'Malcolm' and its sequel 'The Marquis of Lossie,' the scenes of which are laid in the village and its neighbourhood...All the sea and landscape descriptions in Malcolm and its sequel were written after careful observation, and

notes, mental and otherwise, taken on the spot. The essayist said he could picture to himself almost the exact spots where the novelist had stood or sat when looking upon the scenes he had so faithfully and artistically described. They were all familiar to him. He was a well-known figure in the village, and might have been seen night after night repairing to a well-known coign of vantage, the brae head of the village, to gaze in ecstasy upon the brilliant shafts of light emanating from the setting sun...

"Glorious! Glorious!" was all he could ejaculate when he had seen the beautiful visions disappear, and the sombre northern twilight sky take its place. He was passionately fond of looking at the resplendent summer sunsets of this Northern Firth. [13]

13 From *Shields Daily News,* Nov. 27, 1912, reviewing a paper by W. McK Bell "Geo. MacDonald, with some personal reminiscences" delivered before the Shields Literary Institute in England, quoted in *Wingfold* #99, Summer 2017, pp. 41-42.

The visit of 1873

George and Louisa MacDonald returned to Cullen in September of 1873 with daughters Lilia and Grace and family friend and noted social reformer Octavia Hill.

A year after the visit to Cullen recounted above, with the America tour behind them, the time had come to write the long-anticipated story in earnest. MacDonald now returned to Cullen in the autumn of 1873 to work on *Malcolm* more determinedly. On this occasion, George and Louisa were accompanied by Octavia Hill and two of their daughters, Lilia and Grace. It is likely during this visit that they stayed at the Grant Street lodgings where the 1925 bibliography of MacDonald by John Malcolm Bulloch indicates that "*Malcolm* was written." [14] Whether it was a boarding house at the time, a private residence, or what we would today call a "Bed and Breakfast," is unknown. Again MacDonald lectured at the Cullen Town Hall (this time on Burns), and during their visit they were apparently again provided a key to Cullen House.

One cannot but tingle at the thought of George MacDonald sitting in Cullen House while he dreamed up Malcolm's story in his fertile imagination, or in a room of their lodgings on Grant Street, turning that very house into the home of his fictional Miss Horn.

Indeed, it is there on the lower slope of Grant Street that Malcolm's story opens, a dead body lying in an upstairs room when Mrs. Catanach arrives from her house further up the hill on the corner of Grant and Castle streets (what we call "Catanach Corner"), hoping to surreptitiously view the remains.

It is little wonder that Cullen is alive with the spirit of MacDonald. Everywhere you turn, even today, one is confronted with echoing passages from the book. One wonders if the hard Scots mistress of their lodgings, as Louisa described her in a letter home, formed the basis for the character of Miss Horn. (This conjecture is purely my own and contradicts MacDonald's own assertion in the footnote he added in Chapter 42 of *Malcolm* in which he says that he did *not* base the characters in the book on

---

14 Bulloch, *Bibliography*, p. 705.

any real people.) Meanwhile, it is not hard to picture MacDonald sitting across the room from his wife, while Louisa was writing her letter, opening his story by describing the very house they were staying in.

In that letter home, Louisa described the early days of their arrival for their 1873 visit.

Letters from Cullen from Louisa MacDonald

> *Sept. 2, 1873.*
> *These lodgings looked deplorable & the bedrooms are really dismal enough—but the woman is obliging tho' Scotch & hard. The beach is grand as it used to be—the rocks as fine—the Seafield grounds as beautiful, the people about us as kind as ever. We had a long walk this morning. Grace & I sat under the rocks while the others went out and talked to the Port Nockie fishermen. Grace reads me to sleep from the Saturday Review.*
> *Miss Hill is very interesting…Papa oh! so jolly & bright & happy…Papa was taken for Lord Seafield yesterday.* [15]

Louisa later describes a visit to Findlater Castle, which plays such a spooky role in *Malcolm*.

> *Sept. 6, 1873.*
> *We have had a long time today at Findlater Castle & Grace & Miss Hill have been sketching it. We are all sleepy but we are all getting through. The air is cold but very bracing. I should like to send lots of love to you all—I should like to look at you all tonight.*
> *We drove to Findlater or rather were driven—in a dog cart. Six in a dog cart! We had biscuits & bread & cheese for lunch up there—then at four o'clock we walked to Mr. Forbane's house & Mrs. F. brought us all tumblers of what she called milk but it was more cream than milk & brought bread and butter. Harvest bread is only made at harvest time. The fields we came through were so pretty, full of women binding the sheaves & four men cutting corn. It was so pretty but I'm so tired. I can't tell you how nice it was.* [16]

A letter from Octavia Hill to her sister Emily gives a picture of 1873 Cullen through another set of eyes.

---

15 Letter from Cullen: Louisa MacDonald to daughter Mary, Sept. 2, 1873, quoted in *Wingfold* #80, p. 8.
16 Letter from Cullen: Louisa MacDonald to daughter Mary, Sept. 6, 1873, quoted in *Wingfold* #80, p. 8.

Letter about Cullen from Octavia Hill, Sept. 6, 1873

...As to me I am as well as it is possible to be, and very happy. We had magnificent weather for our journey; and here the weather is very nice, tho' we have hardly had a day without some rain. We don't pay any attention to it, but manage to be out seven or eight hours daily. The sea is so grand just now; there have been storms out at sea; and the swell sends the waves rolling in, and breaking in masses of foam about the rocks. There was a revival here among the fishermen twelve years ago; the effects of it seem really to have lasted; and everyone dates all the reforms from that. The fishermen are a splendid race here; vigorous and simple. Mr. MacDonald seems so at home with them; and we often get into nice talks with them on the beach. The sea-town, as they call it, and another tiny village called Port Nochie contain nothing but fishermen; they hardly intermarry at all with the land populations; but are a distinct race, tho' within a few yards of us here. They have only about six surnames in the place; every man is known by a nick-name. We spent the day on Wednesday at an old castle on a promontory of rock, washed on three sides by the sea itself. The position and plan remind me forcibly of Tintagel. It is called Finlater[sic.] *Castle, and is now nothing but a ruin. The family is merged in that of the present Lord Seafield, who is head of the clan Grant; and bears for his motto, 'Stand fast Craig Ellachie!' Do you remember Ruskin's allusion to it in 'The Two Paths'? Lord Seafield's house is close to here. They are away; but have lent Mr. MacDonald keys to the garden and house...* [18]

On Sunday, Sept. 14, 1873, MacDonald preached in Cullen's Independent Chapel. A transcript of the sermon appeared two days later in the Banffshire Journal.

From the *Banffshire Journal,* Sept. 16, 1873 on MacDonald's sermon in the Cullen Independent Chapel

Dr. George MacDonald, the poet and novelist, has been for the last ten days staying at Cullen. On Sunday evening he conducted a public religious service in the Independent Chapel. The small chapel was comfortably filled and there were a number of strangers who had come from a distance to be present.

---

17 The revival mentioned was fictionalised in detail in *Malcolm*, beginning with the chapter entitled "The Revival."
18 Letter from Cullen: Octavia Hill, travelling with the MacDonalds, to her sister Emily Maurice, Sept. 6, 1873, from C. Edmund Maurice, *Life of Octavia Hill as Told in Her Letters* (London: Macmillan, 1913), p. 290; quoted in *Wingfold* #80, pp. 8-9.

Dr. MacDonald gave out as a text John ix, 42 [sic, iv]*...He said:—*

At first sight it seems as if this were not a very gracious speech to make to the woman who had brought to them the good news...But whether it was a bit of bad manners to those people or not, there is a truth in it that belongs to us all. How many of us suppose that we believe in Christ just because we are holding the doctrines that our parents, and schoolmasters, and clergymen, have taught us? A kind of belief that will not stand the least puff of wind from any windy doctrine that sweeps through the world...

Dr. MacDonald went on to advise his hearers first to comprehend the tale—to see what was in it, and then verify the tale by coming to Christ...

He went on to impress the duty of being with God at all times...Our Lord was not ready to speak to everybody. There are foolish people who think of making other people religious by boring them with their talk. Our Lord knew when to be silent and when to speak. He did not take every opportunity of preaching to men by any means...

Dr. MacDonald went on to remark that the whole design of Christ's acting was to do in small things, in comprehensive little pictures, substantially what God is always doing upon the vast scale of the universe. Give me to drink, said the Saviour to the woman. Come and worship me, give me something of your service, says God to man...

Dr. M. then spoke of what salvation consists in. Until a man is so filled with God that God and he are one, that man is not saved; he may be upon the way to be saved. Eternal life is the power of loving our neighbour as ourself, and the power of loving God with our whole being...Eternal Life is not a continuity of existence, but a right condition of the heart towards God. It is oneness with God. And then no man can die. He lives for ever, true; but he lives for ever in virtue of this only, that God dwells in him, and he in God.
19

On Monday, Sept. 15, 1873, MacDonald lectured on Robert Burns in Cullen's Town Hall. The lecture was reported on by both

19 The *Banffshire Journal,* Sept. 16, 1873, quoted in *Wingfold* # 80, pp. 17-23—Excerpts of article and sermon only; complete article reprinted in *Wingfold.* Appreciation goes to John McNeill for his research confirming the Reidhaven Street location of the Independent Chapel.

the *Banffshire Journal* and the *Elgin Courant*, as well as mentioned in a letter by Louisa.

From the *Banffshire Journal*, Sept. 16, 1873 on MacDonald's Burns lecture in the Cullen Town Hall, quoting MacDonald's introduction

Ladies and gentlemen, I have to thank you for the honour...to introduce to you Dr. George MacDonald...He is a luminary of the intellectual firmament...whose moral rays have largely ministered to the delight and instruction of mankind at large. When I had the honour of presiding in this place last year, and on a similar occasion...I took the liberty of expressing the hope, that if he had at all enjoyed his brief sojourn in our Royal Burgh as a place of recreation, that pleasure might lead to his again honouring us with a visit. In that hope we have not been disappointed— [Cheers]—and we hail his return with the delight and enthusiasm due such a visitor. [Great cheering] Since he last addressed us from this platform, he has crossed and re-crossed the Atlantic, and, like a prudent man, in good company—viz., that of his better half. [Laughter and cheers] We rejoice in his successful career among our American cousins, who, I guess, he charmed and electrified...We rejoice in his safe return to his native land, and to the bosom of his family. We rejoice with pride in his following the example of King Robert the Bruce, by selecting Cullen as a favourite and occasional residence...As Scotchmen, we naturally and justly feel proud of a countryman who has done such honour to Scotland...and whose writings have deservedly raised for him a reputation which places him among the elite of our modern authors... [20]

The MacDonalds had apparently had an unpleasant visit from relatives (George still had many in the area). Louisa wrote both about this and her husband's Burns lecture.

Letter from Louisa MacDonald, Sept. 16, 1873

Tuesday, September 16, 1873.
Sunday was so crowded with walking & churchgoing & chapeling & trying to propitiate our cousins whom we unknowingly offended by being out when they arrived on Sat. morning...

---

20 The *Banffshire Journal,* Sept. 16, 1873, quoted in *Wingfold* # 80, pp. 26-27— Excerpts of introductory remarks by Rev. Henderson, parish minister; complete introduction reprinted in *Wingfold.*

15ᵗʰ I was so ill that I haven't quite got over it yet, but I am better to-night. Papa lectured on Burns—alas! I couldn't go—I was sorry. Yes dear they tell me he did say "here and there" & it produced the desired effect. Every one seemed very much delighted with the lecture—this is so well dear. Isn't it nice? [21]

From the *Elgin Courant*, Sept. 19, 1873 on MacDonald's Burns lecture in the Cullen Town Hall

Dr. MacDonald, who has been staying for the last fortnight in Cullen, very kindly consented to deliver a lecture on behalf of the funds of the Cullen Dorcas Society. The subject he selected was Robert Burns, and the lecture was delivered...within the Town Hall...and, although the weather was unfavourable, the attendance was very large.

In speaking of Burns, Dr. M'Donald said—That a great man is generally found where he is not looked for...Now, to give the reason why we speak so highly of Burns. In the first place he gave literature a fresh start. It was a first principle with him to write not of the Tiber...and Thames...but of the burn trotting past his own cottage door. He was not to praise Elizabeth or Helen of Troy, but the girls washing in the burn hard by. He was to sing of his own country, its ways and peculiarities: these were dear to him from his youth. The scenery around him had brought out his spirit to be glad to sing, and the language he was to use would be that in which his mother had told him tales and ancient stories...

The general lessons taught us by Burns are—1ˢᵗ, That the well being of a man lies not in his circumstances, but in himself...

Burns, 2ndly, teaches us to honour the character of a man. The lecturer here read one of Burns' poems—'A man's a man for a' that,' remarking that were it not blotted slightly by an air of spite, the piece is very nearly perfect.

What did Burns do for Scotland specially?...We are but a small people, and to some little noticeable extent love one another. We are as one great clan, bound together by the memories of childhood and country, by the same literature, and also by the fact that Burns lived amongst us. When he appeared our country was drooping asunder. He made us proud of our country, and since then we have clung more closely to him than before.

The beginning of patriotism lies in our love for our parents, our kindred, and specially of the little bit of soil on which we were born...Love of country is but an extension of the love of family...The most patriotic song in any language is 'Scots wha hae.'

---

21 Letter from Cullen: Louisa MacDonald to daughter Mary, Sept. 16, 1873, quoted in *Wingfold* #80, p. 11, The "here *and* there" reference is to a family discussion about the different responses to Robert Burns in America and Scotland, and how differently MacDonald had framed his remarks on Burns (a frequent topic of his lectures) during his recently completed tour of the United States.

What makes it all the more telling is that he makes it assume the form of history, praising the deeds of our ancestors...

We must now speak of the man himself. Many faults have been laid to his charge, some true and some false...This resolution let us make—we will not judge him...With God let us leave him...

Dr. M'Donald...said how delighted he was to revisit Cullen, a place he knew from five and forty years ago, and he hoped to return for a still longer stay. He wished to make one personal statement, that he was about to have, in a serial form, a story, in which would appear descriptions of the scenery of Cullen, but the audience must understand that the characters were altogether ideal, and not real. He should be annoyed if they fixed on any person, as that was not his intention. [22] *Dr. M'Donald resumed his seat amid great applause...*

Upwards of eight pounds were realized, we understand, at the door. [23]

After their return home to England later that autumn, Louisa implies that her husband was homesick for Cullen.

Papa is very poorly. He ought to go to Cullen for a week I think. All his life is gone again—he never smiles and he looks quite as miserable as he did before we went to Scotland. [24]

Whenever and wherever MacDonald carried out the various stages of the writing of *Malcolm*, he apparently struggled with it more than usual. This is surprising because of how skilfully constructed the narrative is. But he was scarcely halfway through

---

[22] MacDonald's closing disclaimer about his forthcoming book was no doubt prompted by the controversy stirred up in Huntly after publication of *Robert Falconer*. Some years before, his own uncle had protested against MacDonald being allowed to preach in Huntly. About this uncle, Greville MacDonald adds: "Twelve years later, when *Robert Falconer* began to appear serially in *The Argosy*, he wrote sternly to its author on the grounds that so many of its characters were portraits and would give offence. He even drove his gig post-haste to Banff to warn the editor of the admirable *Banffshire Journal* against reviewing it."—*George MacDonald and His Wife*, p. 242. MacDonald reinforced the point made at the Burns lecture when *Malcolm* was published a year later, with the following footnote in Chapter 45: "Ill, from all artistic points of view, as such a note comes in, I must, for reasons paramount to artistic considerations, remind my readers, that not only is the date of my story half a century or so back, but, dealing with principles, has hardly anything to do with actual events, and nothing at all with persons. The local skeleton of the story alone is taken from the real, and I had not a model, not to say an original, for one of the characters in it—except indeed Mrs. Catanach's dog."

[23] The *Elgin Courant* Sept. 19, 1873, quoted in *Wingfold* # 80, pp. 29-33—Excerpts only; complete article reprinted in *Wingfold*.

[24] Letter from Louisa to Octavia Hill, October 5, 1873 after return from Cullen, quoted in *Wingfold* #95, Summer 2016, p. 43.

the writing by the end of that year. He pushed through however, and *Malcolm* was serialised through 1874 in the *Glasgow Weekly Herald.*

The complete MacDonald family, 1876, together with prospective son-in-law E. R. Hughes. Top row: Grace, Greville, Mother, Lilia, Ted Hughes, middle row: Ronald, Robert Falconer, Irene, Father, MacKay, Mary, bottom row: Maurice, Winifred, Bernard

"A Story of the Seashore"

Malcolm's compelling story has its origins in the 1830s when as a boy MacDonald formed a lifelong affection for the village of Cullen. MacDonald's poem about Cullen, "A Story of the Seashore," probably first written in the 1850s, is too lengthy to reproduce in full. The Introduction to the poem's "tale" is fully evocative of Cullen as MacDonald describes a visit with his cousin Frank, with whom he grew up on the family farm at Huntly, and their encounter with a childhood friend who told them the eerie legend of Findlater Castle. By the time MacDonald came to write *Malcolm*, the Findlater legend had changed considerably. But the poem remains forever illustrative of MacDonald's affection for the north, his love of his father, and his fond memories of both Huntly and Cullen. If the roots of *Robert Falconer* go back to the late 1850s, the roots of *Malcolm* extend even deeper into George MacDonald's fibre of being. (Another story bearing similarities to the poem in a few respects, probably also based on Cullen and the surrounding region, is "A Child's Holiday" from *Adela Cathcart*.)

Anyone who knows Cullen and its environs will recognise MacDonald's imagery in nearly every line of the poem—the colour of sky and sea, the flowers, the rocky coastline, the beach, the "Temple of Psyche," the fishermen's cottages, and of course the ruins of Findlater. MacDonald's memory of Cullen's details was remarkably vivid. Reproducing this portion of the lengthy poem illustrates perhaps better than any other example MacDonald's propensity to edit and change his work. A more thorough discussion of it is found in the Cullen Collection introduction to *Ranald Bannerman's Boyhood*, as well those of *Castle Warlock* and *Donal Grant*. In this case, anyone who reads "A Story of the Seashore" in its 1857 version in *Poems*, repeated in 1863 in *A Hidden Life*, will find a *completely* different poem than what follows. The two are virtually unrecognizable in places as being the same poem at all.

I quote here from the version MacDonald almost entirely rewrote for Volume 2 of the 1871 publication of *Works of Fancy and Imagination,* which is also reproduced in Volume 1 of *The Poetical Works of George MacDonald* (1893). I quote from that version simply because it would have been written in closer proximity to MacDonald's writing of *Malcolm* than the 1857/63 version.

A Story of the Seashore
"Introduction"

I sought the long clear twilights of my home,
Far in the pale-blue skies and slaty seas,
What time the sunset dies not utterly,
But withered to a ghost-like stealthy gleam,
Round the horizon creeps the short-lived night,
And changes into sunrise in a swoon.
I found my home in homeliness unchanged:
The love that made it home, unchangeable,
Received me as a child, and all was well.
My ancient summer-heaven, borne on the hills,
Once more embraced me; and once more the vale,
So often sighed for in the far-off nights,
Rose on my bodily vision, and, behold,
In nothing had the fancy mocked the fact!
The hasting streams went garrulous as of old;
The resting flowers in silence uttered more;
The blue hills rose and dwelt alone in heaven;
Householding Nature from her treasures brought
Things old and new, the same yet not the same,
For all was holier, lovelier than before;
And best of all, once more I paced the fields
With him whose love had made me long for God
So good a father that, needs-must, I sought
A better still, Father of him and me.

Once on a day, my cousin Frank and I
Sat swiftly borne behind the dear white mare
That oft had carried me in bygone days
Along the lonely paths of moorland hills;
But now we sought the coast, where deep waves foam
'Gainst rocks that lift their dark fronts to the north.
And with us went a girl, on whose kind face
I had not looked for many a youthful year,
But the old friendship straightway blossomed new.
The heavens were sunny, and the earth was green;
The large harebells in families stood along
The grassy borders, of a tender blue
Transparent as the sky, haunted with wings
Of many butterflies, as blue as they.
And as we talked and talked without restraint,
Brought near by memories of days that were,
And therefore are for ever; by the joy
Of motion through a warm and shining air;
By the glad sense of freedom and…the bond of friendship…

I had returned to childish olden time,
And asked her if she knew a castle worn,
Whose masonry, razed utterly above,

Yet faced the sea-cliff up, and met the waves:—
'Twas one of my child-marvels; for, each year,
We turned our backs upon the ripening corn,
And sought some village on the Moray shore;
And nigh this ruin, was that I loved the best.

For oh the riches of that little port!—
Down almost to the beach, where a high wall
Inclosed them, came the gardens of a lord,
Free to the visitor with foot restrained—
His shady walks, his ancient trees of state;
His river—that would not be shut within,
But came abroad, went dreaming o'er the sands,
And lost itself in finding out the sea;

Inside, it bore grave swans, white splendours—crept
Under the fairy leap of a wire bridge...
It was my childish Eden; for the skies
Were loftier in that garden, and the clouds
More summer-gracious, edged with broader white;
And when they rained, it was a golden rain
That sparkled as it fell—an odorous rain.
And then its wonder-heart!—a little room,
Half-hollowed in the side of a steep hill,
Which rose, with columned, windy temple crowned,
A landmark to far seas. The enchanted cell
Was clouded over in the gentle night
Of a luxuriant foliage, and its door,
Half-filled with rainbow hues of coloured glass,
Opened into the bosom of the hill.
Never to sesame of mine that door
Gave up its sanctuary; but through the glass,
Gazing with reverent curiosity,
I saw a little chamber, round and high,
Which but to see was to escape the heat,
And bathe in coolness of the eye and brain;
For all was dusky greenness; on one side,
A window, half-blind with ivy manifold,
Whose leaves, like heads of gazers, climbed to the top...
On a low column stood, white, cold, dim-clear,
A marble woman. Who she was I know not—
A Psyche, or a Silence, or an Echo:
Pale, undefined, a silvery shadow, still,
In one lone chamber of my memory,
She is a power upon me as of old.

But, ah, to dream there through hot summer days,
In coolness shrouded and sea-murmurings,
Forgot by all till twilight shades grew dark!
To find half-hidden in the hollowed wall,
A nest of tales, old volumes such as dreams

Hoard up in bookshops dim in tortuous streets!
That wondrous marble woman evermore
Filling the gloom with calm delirium
Of radiated whiteness, as I read!—
The fancied joy, too plenteous for its cup,
O'erflowed, and turned to sadness as it fell.

But the gray ruin on the shattered shore,
Not the green refuge in the bowering hill,
Drew forth our talk that day. For, as I said,
I asked her if she knew it. She replied,
"I know it well. A woman used to live
In one of its low vaults, my mother says."
"I found a hole," I said, "and spiral stair,
Leading from level of the ground above
To a low-vaulted room within the rock,
Whence through a small square window I looked forth
Wide o'er the waters; the dim-sounding waves
Were many feet below, and shrunk in size
To a great ripple." "'Twas not there," she said,
"—Not in that room half up the cliff, but one—
Low down, within the margin of spring tides:
When both the tide and northern wind are high,
'Tis more an ocean-cave than castle-vault."
And then she told me all she knew of her.
It was a simple tale...how many such are told by night,
In fisher-cottages along the shore!

Whether it is accurate to say that *Malcolm* "grew out of" this poem, it is certain that the memories still green from boyhood which produced the poem burst into flower in the two books of Malcolm's story. The Malcolm doublet surely represents the most evocatively true-to-place work from MacDonald's pen, in which the Seatown, the dwellings along Grant Street, Cullen House, and Findlater's eerie legend, all play prominent roles. So too does MacDonald's family ancestry, tracing its roots back to the massacre of Glencoe, and the enmity since that time between the MacDonald and Campbell clans.

Investigating MacDonald's Cullen connections, in particular the lengthy poem "Story of the Seashore" and the story "A Child's Holiday" from *Adela Cathcart*, Barbara Amell, publisher of the periodical *Wingfold*, has uncovered the fascinating account of a strange woman by the name of Isabel Grant from Sandend, a village about three miles east of Cullen and about half a mile from the ruins of Findlater Castle. Her story was surely known by MacDonald, and indeed she may have been the one he fictionalised into the childhood friend, "a girl, on whose kind face I had not looked for many a youthful year," that he mentions in "Story of the Seashore" as telling him and his cousin Frank the legend of Findlater. If the poem is indeed loosely based on the character of Isabel Grant, MacDonald would obviously not have later encountered her as a woman since by that time the real Isabel was dead.

With Barbara's kind permission, I quote the following portions of her article:

Wingfold Winter 2016 included an article about various people who inspired characters in George MacDonald's fiction. I am pleased to be able to add another example to this list, and to provide more information on MacDonald's fiction, both matters relating to his visits to the coastal town of Cullen, Scotland.

As noted in *Wingfold* Winter 2018, George MacDonald received favorable critical notice for his story "A Child's Holiday" from his 1864 novel *Adela Cathcart.* This tale was based upon the MacDonald family's vacation in Cullen north of their hometown of Huntly, when George was young. The *Globe* critic praised MacDonald's "picture, or rather sketch, of the little sea-maiden which it contains." (May 12, 1864.) Thanks to another review of *Adela Cathcart* in the *Banffshire Journal,* we learn that this character was believed to be based upon a real woman.

Young Herbert, the hero of the story, meets a wild little homeless girl on the beach, who speaks of the sea as her mother. Readers are told that she was a survivor of the wreckage of a Dutch ship, and the town's residents believed her to be "of foreign birth and high descent." The *Banffshire Journal* critic shared a lengthy excerpt on Herbert's encounters with the girl in his review of *Adela Cathcart,* prefaced as follows: "Here are some of the incidents at the coast, including, as will be seen, a reference to a character very well known in Portsoy." Following this excerpt, the critic added:

The character alluded to in the above passage is, we are led to believe, Isabel Grant, who was very well known both in Portsoy and Sandend, which places, as well as the old castle of Findlater, are evidently alluded to in the extract. Isabel, or Bell, as she was called, was no foreigner, and in this, as in many other particulars, our author has made full use of the poetic license. Bell was, we believe, a native of Grange, and an unreciprocated affection brought on a mental derangement. She invariably spoke of the sea as 'her mother,' who was always 'roaring' for something from her, and who would never be satisfied until she got herself—which was the case in the end, the poor creature's body being found among the rocks at Cathie [sic], near Sandend. While she was wandering about, everything she could lay hands on she carried off and threw into the sea, and when nothing better could be had, she would gather up sticks and horse offal for that purpose. She has also been known to divest herself of every article of clothing to satisfy the insatiable cravings of her 'greedy mother.' (Banffshire Journal, April 12, 1864.)

...the critic must have intended to refer to Crathie Point, which is east of Cullen and just west of nearby Sandend, about two miles from Cullen...Apparently the jagged rocks at Crathie Point were where Isabel Grant's body was found.

While the little girl in 'A Child's Holiday' remains alive and well when Herbert and his family leave for home, it is of interest that MacDonald described Herbert seeing the place where Isabel would meet her end. Herbert is taken out in a rowboat by some fishermen in the area, and they row past the ruins of Findlater Castle east of Cullen, where Herbert sees the little girl playing. As the boat moves farther east, 'Herbert looked up with dread at the great cliffs that rose perpendicularly out of the water, which heaved slowly and heavily, with an appearance of immense depth, against them. Their black jagged sides had huge holes, into which the sea rushed—far into the dark—with a muffled roar; and large protuberances of rock, bare and threatening.'

The information on Isabel Grant provides important insights into George MacDonald's poem "A Story of the Sea-Shore." This poem was to my knowledge first published in *A Hidden Life and Other Poems,* released in November 1864; *Adela Cathcart* was first released in March 1864. MacDonald made many changes to 'Sea-Shore' for his 1893 *Poetical Works,* but both versions of the poem take the unusual format of two parts: "Introduction" and "The Story." In the Introduction for the 1864 version, MacDonald described returning to his boyhood home in Huntly for a summer, and spending time there with his father...MacDonald described going for a ride with his cousin Frank and meeting a woman he had known as a youth. They talk of Cullen: "For, each year,/ We turned our backs upon the ripening corn,/ And sought the borders of the desert sea"...It seems possible that MacDonald may have heard when young some sort of legend about a girl in Cullen, which had been altered from the original facts. The portion of the conversation about MacDonald's written story and its differences from the actual woman Isabel was not used in the version of 'Sea-Shore' for *Poetical Works.*

In the version of "Sea-Shore" for *Poetical Works*, MacDonald provided a more detailed description of where Isabel's body was found than he did in the 1864 version...

Wingfold Fall 2012 was devoted to George MacDonald's research visits to Cullen for the novel *Malcolm* in 1872 and 1873. *Malcolm* would begin serialization in the *Glasgow Weekly Herald* in January 1874. A report of MacDonald's lecture on Robert Burns given in Cullen September 15, 1873...quoted him informing the audience that he had set a story in their area, but all the characters were fictional. MacDonald repeated this claim in a footnote for the novel, the sole exception, he added, being a dog. Another report of MacDonald's closing remarks at the 1873 Cullen lecture was recently located:

> *On Monday evening Dr. Macdonald*[sic] *delivered a lecture on 'Robert Burns' in Cullen. In replying to a vote of thanks at the close of the lecture, he said:—I want to tell you a little fact for a certain reason attached to it. I am writing a story just now which will begin to appear soon. If it were coming out in a book all at once I should not say this, because I should have put a little preface to it, though I am afraid most of you would not have read it. But the scene of this story is laid here (Cullen). I wanted to say this because you will recognise at once all the scenery and surroundings. Of course I have to make a little change here and there. But there is not a single real character in the whole book. I am always afraid of anybody supposing that I make living characters. It is all a make up. From the beginning to end there is no foundation for the story either. But I trust that it will not be found to be deficient in that which no story could be without—it ought to be true to human nature. Nothing can pardon any aberration from that. (Ballymena Observer,* October 4, 1873.) [25]

View of Cullen from the Castle Hill

25 From *Wingfold* Summer, 2018. Barbara's Amell's full account of the story of Isabel Grant and her conjectures about the connection to MacDonald's poem can be found in various editions of *Wingfold.*

Later Accounts, Memories, and Tributes

From the *Banffshire Journal* on the occasion of MacDonald's death, 1905

Dr. MacDonald's personality became known to many throughout the North as a gifted lecturer. In many towns throughout the north-eastern counties the appearance of the gifted singer and novelist was hailed as one of the events of the season. We may recall an occasion in 1873 when he lectured at Cullen on Burns for the purpose of noting that in acknowledging a vote of thanks he remarked that a serial story by him, the scene of which was laid at Cullen, would shortly appear. Need we say that he referred to those books which exercise a fascination on young and old—'Malcolm,' and 'The Marquis of Lossie,' in which Cullen and district and its people are so beautifully idealized. [26]

From Daniel Holmes' *Literary Tours of the Highlands and Islands of Scotland*, 1909

It is pleasant to read books amid the scenery in which they were conceived, and among the people they portray. Those who spend their holidays at Cullen would act wisely in reading George Macdonald's [sic—and l.c. "d" continues through article] *novels there. No one has drawn the character of the Moray Firth fishermen so lovingly, beautifully, and sympathetically as he. After reading such a tale as The Marquis of Lossie one looks upon places like Portknockie and the sea-town of Cullen with different eyes. The toilers of the deep that go forth on the waters from these seaboard shires are serious and moral men...Most of the crews carry a box of choice books with them for their odd hours of leisure...Let a stranger get into conversation with one or more of these hardy heroes, and he will be surprised at their intelligence and wide interests. He will certainly conclude that the young fisherman, Malcolm Macphail* [sic.], *whom Macdonald introduces in the novel mentioned, is no exaggeration, but true to the life.*

The sea-town of Cullen consists of some hundreds of houses closely huddled together just at the edge of the sea. The rank odour of wreck [sic.—"wrack," seaweed], *tar, fishing-gear, and bait pervades the air, and is effectively kept from corruption by the searching sea-breezes that are ever blowing. When not engaged on the water, the men are busy mending their nets, stitching their sails, making fast the seams of their craft and taming the big inflated floaters that support the lines.*

---

26 Obituary of George MacDonald, the *Banffshire Journal,* Sept. 19, 1905, quoted in *Wingfold* #80, p. 11.

When the fishing season is over and the crews are known to be on the way home, the excitement among the women is intense...Rarely does a season pass without bringing sorrow to the heart of some waiting wife or sister.

The joys, hopes, and fears of these maritime townships have been worthily made vocal by Dr. George Macdonald. He has done this with a grace and an artistic conception that raise his stories to a very high rank in pure literature. I am afraid Macdonald is not much read by the present generation: his stories are too long, too philosophical, perhaps too poetical, for the taste of to-day. Every book of his is saturated from beginning to end with the religion of the Gospels—a religion of love, beauty, tolerance, and sympathy.

I am happy to say that I saw Dr. Macdonald once and heard him speak. His venerable aspect and chaste elocution made a powerful impression on all who heard him. His discourse could not be reported in cold print, for the flash of the mystic's eye, the human kindness that emanated from his whole being, and the felt emotion of his every tone could not be reproduced by any artifice known to the printer...

WRITTEN AT CULLEN

God will not suffer that a single one
Of His own creatures, in His image made
Should die, and in irrevocable shade
Lie evermore—neglected and undone.

It is not thus a father treats his son,
And those whose folly credits it degrade
God's love and fatherhood, that never fade,
By lies as base as devils ever spun.

Man's love is but a pale reflex of God's,
And God IS love, and never will condemn
Beyond remission—though He school with rods—
His children, but will one day comfort them.
Dives will have his drink at last, and stand
Among the faithful ones at God's right hand. [27]

---

27 Daniel Turner Holmes, *Literary Tours of the Highlands and Islands of Scotland*, Andrew Gardner, Paisley, 1909. This untitled poem (which Holmes gave the dubious title "Dr. George Macdonald's Creed") appeared in *Literary Tours* but does not appear ever to have been published elsewhere among MacDonald's poetical works. MacDonald may have written it for someone in Cullen, but nothing of its origins is known. Article and poem quoted in *Wingfold* #80, pp. 35-37.

From Ronald MacDonald's 1911 remembrance of his father

In a literary life of some forty-two years...George MacDonald produced some fifty-two volumes; of which twenty-five may be classed as novels, three as prose fantasies, eight as tales and allegories for children, five as sermons, three as literary and miscellaneous critical essays, and three as collections of short stories; and five volumes of verse...

This in itself, I think, is a great day's work; and it was accomplished under the strain of a very large family...it was combined with the periodical delivery of lectures...with the editorship of a magazine...while his Sundays in many years were filled with preaching from the pulpits of any who might invite him. After his abandonment of the predicant profession, he never took remuneration for a spoken sermon; and never, I am sure, refused his preaching, from whatever Christian denomination the invitation might come...

Once I asked him why he did not, for change and variety, write a story of mere human passion and artistic plot. He replied that he would like to write it...and went on to tell me that, having begun to do his work as a Congregational minister, and having been driven, by causes here inconvenient to be stated, into giving up that professional pulpit, he was no less impelled than compelled to use unceasingly the new platform whence he had found that his voice could carry so far. [28]

Through stories of everyday Scottish and English life, whose plot, consisting in the conflict of a stereotyped theology with the simple human aspiration toward the divine...he found himself touching the hearts and stimulating the consciences of a congregation never to be herded into the largest and most comfortable of Bethels....

In George MacDonald's blood the Gael at least preponderated very largely; and I cannot doubt that the tradition which existed in his family of escape from the Glencoe massacre affected his imagination strongly, giving him a heart equally open to the Highland and the Lowland appeal.

In the main it is the Saxon Scot, whom from childhood he best knew, that he shows us in the best of his novels; but his occasional picture of a Highlander will stand out from the canvas with great distinction; and it may be doubted whether he ever equalled in clarity of characterization or profundity of loving humour his Duncan MacPhail, the blind piper of Portlossie. In his lofty, yet half savage sense of honour, his feminine tenderness, his berserk fits of rage, his jubilant piping...in his noble lament for Glencoe...is at once the type of the Celt for his author, and the

---

28 This response is echoed by Ronald's brother, who commented in his biography, "'People,' he once remarked, 'find this great fault with me—that I turn my stories into sermons. They forget that I have a Master to serve first before I can wait on the public.'" From Greville MacDonald's *George MacDonald and His Wife,* p. 375.

reconstruction (I suggest merely) of the influence upon his author of Highland tradition. [29]

From G.K. Chesterton's 1924 tribute to George MacDonald

The originality of George MacDonald...perhaps can best be estimated by comparing him with his great countryman Carlyle...Carlyle never lost the Puritan mood even when he lost the whole of the Puritan theology. If an escape from the bias of environment be the test of originality, Carlyle never completely escaped, and George MacDonald did. He evolved out of his own mystical meditations a complete alternative theology...Carlyle could never have said anything so subtle and simple as MacDonald's saying that God is easy to please and hard to satisfy. Carlyle was too obviously occupied with insisting that God was hard to satisfy; just as some optimists are doubtless too much occupied with insisting that He is easy to please. In other words, MacDonald had made for himself a sort of spiritual environment, a space...of mystical light which was quite exceptional in his national and denominational environment...And when he comes to be more carefully studied...it will be found, I fancy, that he stands for a rather important turning-point in the history of Christendom, as representing the particular Christian nation of the Scots...

The spiritual colour of Scotland, like the local colour of so many Scottish moors, is a purple that in some lights can look grey. The national character is in reality intensely romantic and passionate...

The passionate and poetical Scots ought obviously...to have had a religion which competed with the beauty and vividness of the passion, which did not let the devil have all the bright colours, which fought glory with glory and flame with flame...

Now, among the many men of genius Scotland produced in the 19th century, there was only one so original as to go back to this origin. There was only one who really represented what Scottish religion should have been... In his particular type of literary work he did indeed realize the apparent paradox of a St. Francis of Aberdeen, seeing the same sort of halo round every flower or bird...To have got back to it, or forward to it, at one bound of boyhood, out of the black Sabbath of a Calvinist town, was a miracle of imagination. [30]

---

29 Ronald MacDonald "George MacDonald: A Personal Note," Chapter 3 of *From a Northern Window*: "Papers, Critical, Historical and Imaginative."
30 G.K. Chesterton, in the "Introduction" to *George MacDonald and His Wife* by Greville MacDonald, pp. 12-14..

From the *Illustrated Guide Book of Cullen and District,* 1931

> *Cullen House, the stately castle home of the Seafields, must be quite familiar to many a person who has never seen it, but who has read George MacDonald's companion volumes, 'Malcolm' and 'The Marquis of Lossie.' This author so weaves romance and history round the building, brings the animate and inanimate into such vivid connection with it, that it never can be a mere pile of stones and lime, and nothing more.* [31]

From John Matthewman's article in *The Scots Magazine,* 1939

> *During his long life MacDonald wrote many books, and there can be no question that he ranks with Scott and Stevenson as a Scottish classic.*
>
> *Recently I made my way to Aberdeenshire, to the substantial old Burgh of Huntly, which is situated in the heart of the pastoral Gordon country...*
>
> *Evening found me in Cullen, the old royal burgh on the Banffshire coast, which is my headquarters when I am in Moray; not only because I have old friends there but on account of the interest and beauty of the place. George MacDonald chose it for the setting of his best-known novel 'Malcolm,' and its sequel, 'The Marquis of Lossie,' which are to be considered, of course, as one great work. This remarkable book has captivated me more than any other of his stories.*
>
> *The 'Portlossie' of the novel is a faithful reproduction of Cullen, and it was here that the novelist spent several summers, fraternizing with the fishermen and traversing the countryside to gain his local colour...*
>
> *Cullen is handy to that fine countryside which lies between the Moray shore and the great mountains of the interior. Its wilder parts are gorgeous in early summer with the golden broom. When the broom has shed its blossom and the gold is on the cornfields, then there is the added glory of the purple heather, and in these kinder months the sea is strangely blue.*
>
> *The gaunt ruin of the ancient castle of Findlater is but a mile or two away. It was in 1600 that the Ogilvies decided to vacate it, for in that year the building of the stately Cullen House was commenced on the site of a monastery. It is in the Scots baronial style and extends to the edge of a high rock, round whose base flows the beautiful trout stream of Cullen Burn. Within the policies of this great house, fifty miles of woodland paths may be traversed amid beeches and oaks and conifers of a size deemed unlikely in the North.*
>
> *Within the demesne, and close against the house, stands the ancient church, once in line with the Alton or old town of Cullen*

---

31 George W. Findlay, *Illustrated Guide Book of Cullen and District,* 1931.

which has long since passed away. Now one walks to the church beneath an arching canopy of trees, and the borders of the road are rich in springtime with primroses and bluebells. The earliest known mention of this church is in the year 1209. It was originally a rectangular chapel of the Virgin. Seventy years ago a Norman doorway was discovered at the west end, and its arch was restored and converted into a window, and the outer ground was then some feet higher...

Separated alike from the high tower of Cullen and the policies of the House by the main road to the west, the fisher-town of Seaton lies close to the sea, its hundreds of clean-painted cottages a model of quaint irregularity and scrambling juxtaposition. A mile or two to the west, just beyond Scaurnose Head, is the charming and modernized fishing village of Portknockie, the 'Scaurnose' of 'Malcolm.' It is a pleasant walk across the 'links,' that grassy expanse which lies behind the broad bay of Cullen and ultimately mounts up to the elevation of Scaurnose Head, beneath which are peculiar and extensive caves with a history all their own. Away to the eastward at some two leagues distance is Portsoy, on the road to Banff, or 'Dufftown," where the 'Wan Water,' broad and serene, flows into the sea.

Just beyond the tollhouse on the Portsoy road, there is a fine view of the open country away inland, and for a grand seascape one may leave the road by the Crannoch walk and go up through the wood of birches and pass the heather-encircled loch on to the broad cliff-top, along which the path continues to Sunnyside and the Hermit's House. From this vantage-point one may see the ocean stretching away illimitably to the north and east, while far to the west, if the day be clear, the outline of Cromarty Firth and the great stretch of the Sutherland and Caithness coast will be plainly in view.

Amid such a countryside as this George MacDonald wrote his great book of real scenes, real people, and real sentiment.

It is not always summer, however, in this novel. The dark days and falling leaves, the cold storm-driven rain, have their place and their psychological counterpart. Sorrow and mystery are in the first chapter, and weave in and out with joy and wit and pleasant scenes to make the skein of the story. Interest grows with the introduction of characters so diverse that no one but a genius could make them serve his deep, unswerving purpose. [32]

---

32 John Matthewman, *The Scots Magazine,* excerpts, 1939, from *Wingfold,* # 80, p. 40-42.

From C.S. Lewis's 1946 tribute to George MacDonald

George Macdonald's [sic.—and throughout] *family (though hardly his father) were of course Calvinists. On the intellectual side his history is largely a history of escape from the theology in which he had been brought up...*

All his life he continued to love the rock from which he had been hewn. All that is best in his novels carries us back to that 'kaleyard' world of granite and heather, of bleaching greens beside burns that look as if they flowed not with water but with stout, to the thudding of wooden machinery, the oatcakes, the fresh milk, the pride, the poverty, and the passionate love of hard-won learning...

In Macdonald it is always the voice of conscience that speaks. He addresses the will: the demand for obedience, for 'something to be neither more nor less nor other than done' is incessant...The Divine Sonship is the key-conception which unites all the different elements of his thought...I know hardly any other writer who seems to be closer, or more continually close, to the Spirit of Christ Himself...Nowhere else outside the New Testament have I found terror and comfort so intertwined...Inexorability—but never the inexorability of anything less than love—runs through it like a refrain; 'escape is hopeless...the uttermost farthing will be extracted.'...

I have never concealed the fact that I regarded him as my master; indeed I fancy I have never written a book in which I did not quote from him. [33]

33 C.S. Lewis, *George MacDonald An Anthology,* "Preface," Geoffrey Bles, 1946.

George MacDonald:

A Brief Life Sketch
By Michael Phillips

Descended of Clanranald of the ancient Clan Donald of western Scotland, George MacDonald's more recent ancestry traces to the Glencoe massacre of 1692. His great-great-great-grandfather, half-brother of the slain chief of the small Glencoe clan of MacDonald, escaped the glen with his family, migrating north and east along the coast to the small coastal fishing village of Portsoy. His son became a Portsoy quarryman, whose son William became the town piper. This William MacDonald joined Bonnie Prince Charlie in 1745. A son was born to his wife just three months before Culloden. She named him Charles Edward in honour of the bonnie prince for whom her husband was fighting. William was one of the few who escaped with his life. He was chased through Nairn and hid for months in the caves along the coast on his way back to Portsoy, where he rejoined his family and new son. Eventually he lost his eyesight, though resumed his duties and was thereafter known as "the blind piper of Portsoy."

George MacDonald's grandfather, the youngest of the piper's large family, Charles Edward MacDonald, was apprenticed to the weaving business in the growing textile industry, and eventually moved to Huntly, south of Portsoy. There he married Isabella Robertson of Drumblade and built up a successful bleaching (dyeing) and spinning business. Their three sons, George, Charles, and James, inherited the business.

George MacDonald Sr. married Helen MacKay in 1822. Their second son, George MacDonald, Jr., was born on December 10, 1824 in a newly constructed house in Huntly near the corner of Church and Duke Streets, next to the home of young George's grandmother Isabella MacDonald.

Two years later, George Sr. and Helen moved to a new and larger house up from the banks of the Bogie near the MacDonald mill. The new house was originally called "Bleachfield Cottage," but was generally known as the Farm. It was there that young George MacDonald spent his childhood. Many of his later poems and stories have roots in Huntly and its environs.

His mother died when George was eight. He and his brothers were then looked after by relatives of the extended MacDonald family. Grandmother MacDonald, who still lived in the house at the corner of Duke and Church streets in Huntly, occupied an especially formative role. Her fiery Calvinism proved one of the great spiritual influences in young George MacDonald's life, and gave rise to his later transformational theological writings on the Christian faith. Breaking from the Calvinism of his boyhood, an expansive perspective of the nature of God and his loving Fatherhood suffuses all MacDonald's novels and other writings. (George Sr. remarried in 1839. He and his new wife Margaret had three daughters, to whom George was close all his life.)

With cousins and other relatives in Portsoy and Banff, visits by the MacDonald family to the coast north of Huntly were regular, especially after the death of Helen MacDonald in 1832. The earliest remaining writings from George MacDonald's hand are dated during the summers of 1833 and 1834 to his father from Portsoy, where he was staying with his aunt and uncle and cousins. He speaks of swimming in the sea, a dead whale on the shore, visiting the house and castle at Fordyce, and going out in a Prussian schooner which was harboured at Portsoy. His love of the sea is obvious. George's holiday visits to the coast included Cullen. An undated letter when he was eleven or twelve, written from Cullen, Portsoy, or Banff, is almost apologetic in informing his father that he has decided on a career as a sailor: "I must tell you that the sea is my delight and that I wish to go to it as soon as possible, and I hope that you will not use your parental authority to prevent me, as you undoubtedly can. I feel I would be continually wishing and longing to be at sea." [34]

George MacDonald did not go to sea, though his happy memories and abiding affection for Cullen and Portsoy were lifelong. He entered Aberdeen University at sixteen, where he studied Chemistry and Physics. By the time of his graduation, however, after some years wrestling with the strict Calvinism of his childhood to discover a faith of his own, he had decided to enter the ministry. Two years followed at Highbury Theological College in London. Early in 1851, shortly after his 27th birthday, he was called as minister to a small congregational church in Arundel on the south coast of England. Two months later he and Louisa Powell were married.

MacDonald's brief tenure at Arundel would prove to be his first as well as his last pulpit. His imaginative views were unsettling to the working-class congregation. He made the mistake of expressing his belief that animals would share in the afterlife. Even worse were hints detected by some in his congregation that seemed to allow for the possibility of redemption for unbelievers after death. Many women in particular, and most of the church deacons, were scandalised at the implied heresy. Pressure was put on MacDonald to resign, though he

34 Greville MacDonald, *George MacDonald and His Wife*, p. 66.

endured their efforts to oust him for two years. Eventually he bowed to their wishes and resigned in 1853.

MacDonald was already writing by this time. His literary career was launched in 1855 with the publication of a lengthy romantic poem entitled *Within and Without*. Though the next eight years, with a growing family that eventually numbered eleven children, were ones of financial struggle, MacDonald began to gain a reputation among the literati of England. His first book attracted the admiration of Lady Byron, the poet's widow, and Charles Kingsley. As a result, and believing in the young mystic, Lady Byron assisted the MacDonald family financially as she was able. A second volume from MacDonald's hand, simply entitled *Poems*, was published in 1857. It was followed in 1858 by what many consider MacDonald's imaginative masterpiece *Phantastes*. MacDonald was by now attracting wider notice in London, and began to be in demand as a lecturer and preacher. A wide array of associations evidenced MacDonald's rising stature among the eminent personalities of the time—John Scott, John Ruskin, Lord and Lady Mount-Temple, Frederick Denison Maurice, Octavia Hill, Matthew Arnold, Arthur Hughes, Diana Mulock, Margaret Oliphant, and William Thackeray. Charles Dodgson (Lewis Carroll) became a particularly close friend. Indeed, MacDonald's children were the first to listen to a reading of Dodgson's *Alice in Wonderland*. Their reception of it convinced him to publish it.

George MacDonald's career took a major leap forward in 1863 with the publication of his first lengthy realistic Scottish novel, *David Elginbrod*. Its instant success vaulted MacDonald into the lofty regions of best-sellerdom. For the rest of his life he was known as one of the eminent Victorian novelists of the time. Some indication of his renown is represented by the fact that Queen Victoria gave copies of *Robert Falconer* to her grandchildren.

More poetry, many collections of short stories, a half dozen volumes of theological and literary essays, and a ground-breaking study of Hamlet all followed from his prolific pen over the next thirty years. George MacDonald's reputation through the latter four decades of the 19th century, however, rested primarily on his best-selling realistic novels and imaginative children's books. Following *David Elginbrod* came an extraordinary succession of best-sellers: *Robert Falconer* (1867), *At the Back of the North Wind* (1871), and *The Princess and the Goblin* (1872).

In 1872, at the height of his fame, MacDonald returned north to the place of boyhood memories to begin writing what many consider his most towering fictional masterpiece—the doublet *Malcolm* (1875) and *The Marquis of Lossie* (1877).

In the following decades, George MacDonald continued to produce a succession of memorable fantasies and magnificent portrayals of Scottish and English life: *Thomas Wingfold Curate* (1876), *Sir Gibbie* (1879), *Warlock O'Glenwarlock* (1882), *Donal Grant* (1883), *What's Mine's Mine* (1886), and, as a bookend to *Phantastes*, his end of life fantasy *Lilith* (1895). All told, MacDonald produced over fifty volumes of enormous variety. By the time of his death in 1905, he was regarded as one of the most influential of "the Victorians." In his obituary of MacDonald in the *London Daily News,* G.K. Chesterton wrote: "George MacDonald was one of the three or four greatest men of the nineteenth century." [35]

George MacDonald   J. A. Froude   Wilkie Collins   Anthony Trollope
W. M. Thackeray   Lord Macaulay   Bulwer Lytton   Thos. Carlyle   Charles Dickens
GROUP OF CONTEMPORARY WRITERS

35 G.K. Chesterton, Obituary in *The London Daily News,* Sept. 23, 1905, quoted in *George MacDonald, Scotland's Beloved Storyteller* by Michael Phillips, page 344.

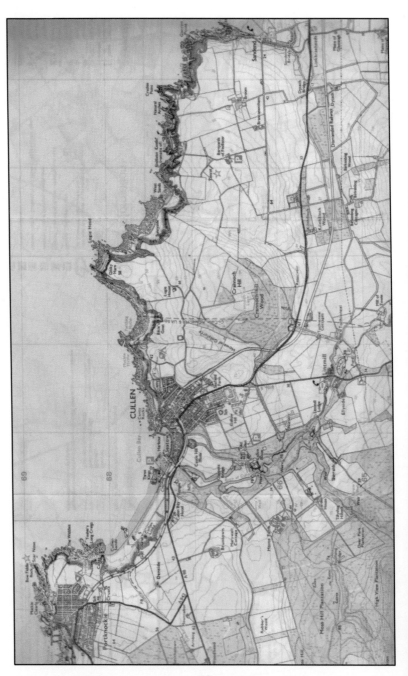

MacDonald Walks Around Cullen
With Judy's Notes

The Scar Nose Loop (4.0 miles)

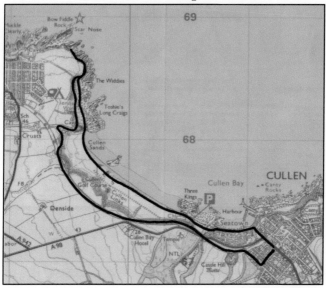

When I have the chance to take MacDonald readers on a walk around Cullen, there is nothing like this loop for an overview of the area. We usually begin by following the old railway line to Portknockie and the Scar Nose and Bow Fiddle overlook—one of my favourite places in all the world—then returning, making our way down the steps and along the beach. So many sites from Malcolm's story come alive on this walk—the beach itself, the long dune, the preacher's cave, Florimel's rock (the "Black Fit"), and of course the Seatown. Also of interest are Jenny's Well and the Whale's Mouth ("Faal's Mou").

The Castle Hill Loop
(1.0 mile)

"The Bothy" (1.75 miles)

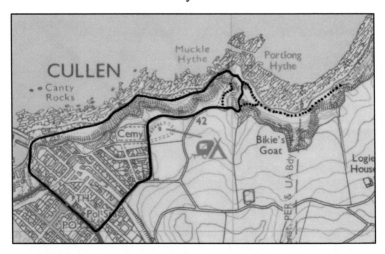

Though there is no longer a salmon bothy (a shared public cottage) in Cullen, it was an important structure in the past where many of the salmon fishermen stayed over the summer months. They pulled their boats up at high tide, and their ramp through the break in the rocks is still visible.

Start at the square and walk up Seafield Street to Seafield Place. Turn left and follow the road to the playground. There the street sweeps around left toward the cemetery and the caravan park. Follow the path along the cemetery wall, then right. After leaving the end of the caravan park and walking bedside thick clumps of bright yellow gorse (blooming in May and early June) or equally yellow Scotch broom (flowering a bit later), a path to the left leads to the overlook of Nelson Point (which Mike used for the climax of *Murder By Quill*). Take a few moments to walk to the edge of the bluff. There you will find benches and a monument with arrows to show the directions and distances to different locations.

Retrace your steps, turn left back onto the path, and continue down the hill toward the site of the old bothy. A bench prior to the descent is one of the best places to sit and take a picture. It was here one summer evening when there was a full moon that a friend was out walking his dog and saw dolphins cavorting in the moonlight in the little bay.

About three-quarters of the way down the hill, a lesser-used path leads off to the right. It takes you on around the bay called Portlong Hythe. You may sit on the bench about midway around the bay, then return to the main path and continue the Bothy Walk. If followed, this trail leads on to Logie Head, the Giant's Steps, the site where Charlie the Hermit lived, Sunnyside Beach, Findlater, and eventually Sandend.

As the Bothy path descends to sea level, enjoy the seasonal wild flowers as you continue your way back toward the harbour. You will see Cullen's unique pet cemetery and then will pass the Cullen Sea School where boats are being built and the skiffs are kept for rowing out into the sea. Continue on past the harbour and up the hill and back to the square.

The Auld Kirk or *Malcolm* "Funeral" Loop (1.3 miles)

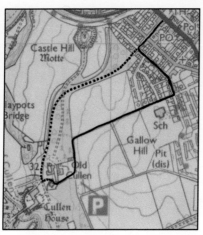

That night the weather changed and grew cloudy and cold. A northeast wind tore off the tops of the drearily tossing billows. All was gray—enduring, hopeless gray. Along the coast the waves kept roaring on the sands, persistent and fateful...

Through the drizzle-shot wind and the fog blown in shreds from the sea, a large number of the most respectable of the male population of the burgh, clothed in Sunday gloom deepened by the crape on their hats, made their way to Miss Horn's...

The sounds of trampling and scuffling feet bore witness that the undertaker, Watty Witherspail, and his assistants were carrying the coffin down the stair. Soon the waiting company rose to follow it and, trooping out, arranged themselves behind the hearse, which, horrid with nodding plumes and gold and black panelling, drew away from the door to make room for them...

The procession began to move...and together they followed in silence, through the gusty wind and monotonous drizzle.

The schoolhouse was close to the churchyard. An instant hush fell upon the scholars when the hearse darkened the windows, lasting while the horrible thing slowly turned to enter the iron gates.

—Malcolm, The Cullen Collection edition, chapter 9

The Cullen House Grounds Loop (2.0 miles)

The Cullen House grounds are open to the public on Tuesday and Friday afternoons from 1:30 to 4:30. One can enter through the Town Gate at the head of Grant Street and stroll the half mile to the magnificent Scots baronial style former residence of Lord Seafield, now privately owned condominium-residences. (Though it looks the part, Cullen House is not technically a "castle" as it was not built for defensive purposes.)

A side walk through a gate in the stone wall takes you to Cullen's Auld Kirk (open from 2:00 to 4:00 on the same days in summer months) or around the House to the bridge over the Cullen Burn. Continuing the loop from the front of the House takes you through the Grand Entry, along its stately tree-lined entry drive, and back into Cullen.

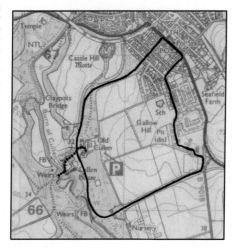

Cullen to Findlater (Out and back, approx. 5 miles)

Pack a picnic (like the MacDonalds did) of bread and cheese and fruit, and plan to spend a good portion of the day for this walk. It is steep and rough in places between Logie Head and Findlater, so don't walk it in rainy or windy weather. You will find lovely Sunnyside beach a wonderful secluded spot for a picnic. The climb from the beach up to the bluff and ruins of Findlater Castle is steep and can be muddy. Be very careful around the ruins and don't get too adventurous. Remember what happened to Florimel! The ruins have deteriorated even more since MacDonald's day and can be treacherous.

If you're not up for the out and back trek, take the 35 bus to either the Dytack or Sandend bus-stop and walk along the road (dotted line) to the Barnyards of Findlater, and thence through the field to the castle ruins. Small signs along the roads point the way to Findlater. A word of caution about returning by bus—the bus between Cullen and Sandend only comes along every hour, and walking along the A 95 is very dangerous.

A Village Lanes and Byways Walk (1.3 miles)

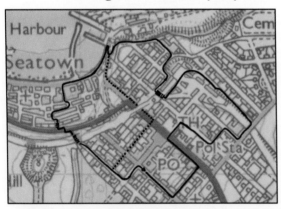

The Scottish coastal village of Cullen along the temperate Moray Firth offered the ideal seaside holiday.

The town and its environs was a relaxed old-fashioned place where visitors came to forget the pace of modern life. Its three busiest shops sold ice cream, fish and chips, and antiques. The setting hardly seemed likely for murder.

A tall and imposing figure strode briskly between rows of gray stone houses. The buildings among which he walked were gray, the street and sidewalk were gray, the roof slates were gray. Once leaving the greenery of the surrounding countryside and entering its cities and towns, gray became the predominant feature of the northern Scottish landscape

The walker had made his way from Cullen House along a half-mile spectacular wooded drive into the village proper. With the crisp gait of the Germanic branch of his ancient Celtic ancestry, he turned into a narrow lane and made his way toward the noisy main thoroughfare through town...

Hugh Barribault continued to the square at the center of town. He stopped briefly at The Paper Shoppe for the day's Telegraph, Times, and Press and Journal from Alan Long. Finally he completed the circle he had begun earlier, walking up Grant Street and again through the gate into the grounds of Cullen House.
—Murder By Quill, Michael Phillips, chapter 1

The Cullen Burn Walk

Claypots Bridge and return (Black—Out and back, 2.0 miles)
Loop through grounds on permitted days (red & black—2.3 mi.)
Or to Temple (dotted black)

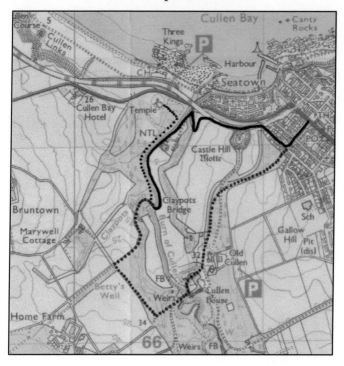

This is one of the most beautiful, varied, and scenic of all the walks, now more accessible thanks to the new path from the top of the viaduct through the field and winding down to the Sea Gate, from which the walk up the side of Cullen Burn to the Claypots Bridge, with Cullen House looming in the distance, is like entering another world. For the intrepid who do not mind a little cross-country traipsing up the final hill, the Temple which figures so prominently in *Malcolm*, can be reached by continuing back along the opposite side of the Burn. It is this route along the Burn to Cullen House that Malcom walked numerous times in the story. Though there is a walking gate through the Sea Gate toward the Seatown, there is no walking pavement, and the traffic coming from the right is completely cut off from sight by the viaduct pillar. (Non U.K. visitors remember: *Look to your right when crossing streets!*) This is a main highway and very busy. This is a treacherous crossing and is not recommended.

Out and Back Walk to *Angel Harp* Bench (7.0 miles)

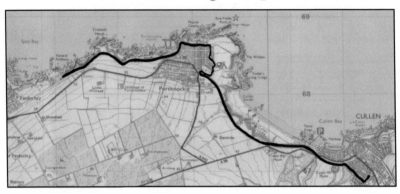

    In the spring of 2009, I happened to be alone at our home in Scotland. Returning from a long bike ride, I stopped a couple miles from home and sat down on a bench high on a bluff overlooking the Moray Firth of the North Sea. It was a spectacular day, breezy but pleasant, the ocean a deep blue. As I sat at the edge of the promontory, a seagull flew past in front of me, drifting on the winds blown upward from the ocean against the cliff face at about the height where I sat. Slowly, as it glided by a few feet in front of me, wings outstretched, the gull's head turned and glanced briefly toward me.

    It was one of those magical moments of "connection" between man and the animal kingdom that brings a joy to the heart. Obviously the gull was not thinking about me as he flew by, but the turn of his head stabbed my senses with undefined pleasure. I imagined him saying, "There is a story waiting to be told about that bench you are sitting on, about this coastline, about that village just there along the path. Mysteries are about to be revealed. I know of them…and you will know of them soon."

    Just as quickly he was gone.

    As I sat staring out to sea, the awe deepened. I was left to ponder the moment and what it might mean. Gradually one of those creative what-ifs began to coalesce in my brain:—

    What if a visitor came to this part of Scotland, came to this very spot, this village…and walked this path along this bluff and sat upon this very bench? What if such a person came here knowing nothing, expecting nothing…and slowly found himself or herself drawn into the life of the community? And what if such a person discovered the story the seagull had to tell?

    That was it.

    A village in Scotland…a path along a bluff…a bench overlooking the sea…and the momentary glance of a Scottish seagull.

    As I continued on my ride toward our home in Cullen a few minutes later, a sentence came to me. I don't know why, or where it came from. I had no idea what it meant, what it might refer to. I had no idea who was speaking it.

    The sentence was:—

    It is a terrible thing when dreams die.

    With nothing more than that, I began to write, just to explore what the mysterious look of the gull might have to say. I would write down that one sentence, and hope that perhaps a second might follow.

    —Michael Phillips, from the "Afterword" of *Angel Harp*

Books, Pamphlets, Brochures of Cullen Interest

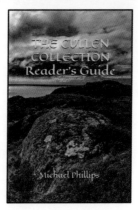

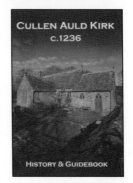

The Cullen Collection

of the Fiction of George MacDonald, updated by Michael Phillips

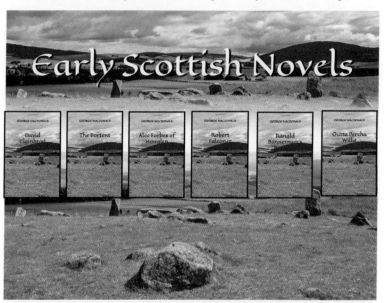

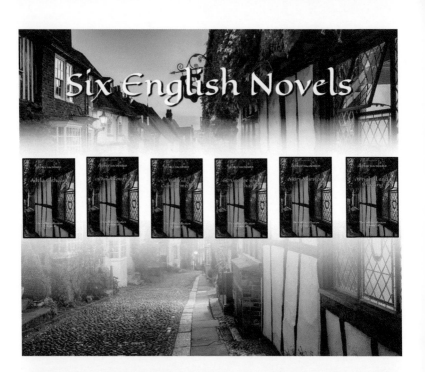

Six English Novels

Two English Trilogies

The Scottish Masterworks

Malcolm	Sir Gibbie	The Marquis of Lossie	Castle Warlock	Donal Grant	What's Mine's Mine

The Short Novels

Home Again — The Elect Lady — A Rough Shaking — The Flight of the Shadow

Heather and Snow — Salted With Fire — Far Above Rubies

Additional copies of
George MacDonald, Cullen, and Malcolm
can be ordered from Amazon.
Discounted bulk orders for ten copies or more
available from Michael and Judy Phillips on
"The Bookstore" @
FatheroftheInklings.com.

Printed in Great Britain
by Amazon

43252301R00046